my revision notes

(17) 2014

AS AQA History
TSARIST RUSSIA
1855–1917

Sally Waller

Series editors:
Robin Bunce
Laura Gallagher

Orders: please contact Bookpoint Ltd, 130 Milton Park, Abingdon, Oxon OX14 4SB.
Telephone: +44 (0)1235 827720. Fax: +44 (0)1235 400454. Lines are open 9.00a.m.–5.00p.m., Monday to Saturday, with a 24-hour message answering service. Visit our website at www.hoddereducation.co.uk.

© Sally Waller 2012
First published in 2012 by
Hodder Education,
an Hachette UK company
338 Euston Road
London NW1 3BH

Impression number 10 9 8 7 6 5 4 3
Year 2016 2015 2014

Cover photo: © Alex_Mac-Fotolia

Typeset in 11/13 Stempel Schneidler Std-Light by Datapage (India) Pvt. Ltd.
Artwork by Datapage (India) Pvt. Ltd.
Printed and bound in India

A catalogue record for this title is available from the British Library.

ISBN 978 1 444 177480

Contents

Introduction

About Unit 1

Unit 1 is worth 50 per cent of your AS level. It requires an understanding of change and continuity over time and an awareness of cause and consequence within a broad historical context. There are no sources in the Unit 1 examination and therefore all marks available are awarded for your own knowledge and understanding.

In the examination, you are required to answer two questions out of three and each question has two parts. The first part, worth 12 marks, asks you to explain why an event, issue or development occurred. 12 mark questions begin 'Explain why' or 'Why did'. The second part, worth 24 marks, requires a balanced evaluation and begins 'How far', 'How important' or 'How successful'. The examination lasts for 1 hour and 15 minutes, unless you have been awarded extra time. You are advised to spend 12 minutes on the first part of each question and 25 minutes on the second part.

The examination will test your own knowledge and understanding of the period and requires you to:

- refer to relevant historical information
- demonstrate an understanding of change and continuity
- show an awareness that events and developments are open to differing interpretations
- use good English, organise information clearly and use specialist vocabulary where appropriate.

Tsarist Russia 1855–1917

The specification lists the content of Unit 1: Tsarist Russia, 1855–1917 under the following broad headings:

1. Reform and reaction, 1855–1881
2. Political reaction: social and economic change, 1881–1904
3. Russia in Revolution, 1904–1906
4. The Tsarist regime, 1906–1914
5. The First World War and the revolutions of 1917

How to use this book

This book has been designed to help you to develop the knowledge and skills necessary to succeed in the examination of this unit. The book is divided into five sections – one for each section of the unit. Each section is made up of a series of topics organised into double-page spreads. On the left-hand page, you will find a summary of the key content you need to learn. Words in bold in the key content are defined in the glossary (see pages 64–66). On the right-hand page, you will find exam-focused activities. Together, these two strands of the book will provide you with the knowledge and skills essential for examination success.

▼ Key historical content   ▼ Exam-focused activities

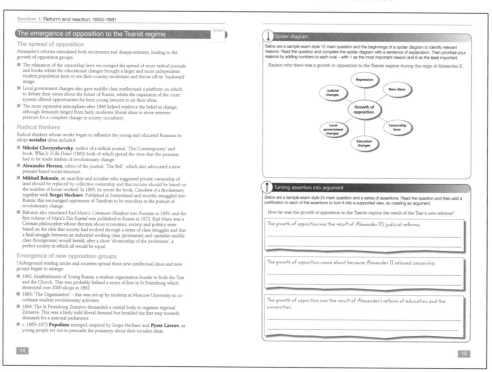

There are two types of examination activities focusing on the two types of examination questions.

- 'Explain why' and 'Why did' 12 mark questions have this symbol:
- 'How far', 'How important' and 'How successful' 24 mark questions have this symbol:

The activities have answers or suggested answers on pages 68–78.

Each section ends with an exam-style question and model A-grade answer with examiner's commentary. This will give you guidance on what is expected in order to achieve the top grade.

You can also keep track of your revision by ticking off each topic heading in the book, or by ticking the checklist on the contents page. Tick each box when you have:

- revised and understood a topic
- completed the activities.

Mark scheme

For some of the activities in the book it will be useful to refer to the mark scheme for the unit. Below is an abbreviated form of the mark scheme for Unit 1.

Assessing 'Explain why' and 'Why did' questions			
Level and marks	Approach	Detail	Understanding
Level 1 1–2	Descriptive/generalised		
Level 2 3–6	Descriptive or limited (1–2 factors)	Little supporting evidence	
Level 3 7–9	Range of factors (usually 3+)	Some supporting evidence	
Level 4 10–12	Range of factors (usually 3+)	Precise supporting evidence	Makes links between factors

Assessing 'How far', 'How important' and 'How successful' questions				
Level and marks	Knowledge	Understanding	Balance of interpretations	Judgement
Level 1 1–6	Limited detail or little description	Generalised comment or assertion		
Level 2 7–11	Some detail or some description	Some (limited) explicit links or comment		
Level 3 12–16	Suitable detail/lacks depth	Explicit links/lacks weight	Maybe some balance	
Level 4 17–21	Good range of detail showing depth	Explicit understanding	Balanced argument	
Level 5 22–24	Precise detail	Explicit understanding	Well-balanced argument	Judgement

Section 1:
Reform and reaction, 1855–1881

Alexander II's motives for reform

Background

Mid-nineteenth century Russia was a large but economically underdeveloped empire with a ratio of 11:1 village to town dwellers. Around 85 per cent of the population were illiterate **peasants**, mostly either privately or state-owned **serfs**. Most serfs belonged to village communes, or **mirs**, where their village elders regulated their primitive **strip-farming**. They paid their master for the land in rent or labour and could be bought, sold and beaten by him.

Ruling over Imperial Russia was an **autocratic Tsar** who was also the head of the Russian Orthodox Church. He was believed to possess semi-divine powers. His edicts (or **Ukase**) were law and he could choose his own advisers.

The Crimean War

Alexander II became Tsar in March 1855. Russia was in the final stage of a disastrous war in the Crimea (north of the Black Sea). They had been fighting the British there since 1853 and had suffered several defeats, including the Battles of Balaclava and Inkerman in 1854. In August 1855, they lost Sebastopol, a major naval base. The final defeat in 1856 highlighted both the problem of Russia's reliance on serf armies (where harshly treated **conscripts** served for 25 years) and the country's economic backwardness, particularly its lack of railways and outdated weaponry. Despite spending 45 per cent of annual expenditure on the army, Russia suffered incompetent officers, humiliation and an increase in serf uprisings.

Alexander II's views

Having travelled the Empire, served on his Father's **Council of State** and led a **serfdom** committee, Alexander II believed in serf **emancipation** to curb tensions and stimulate the economy. His brother,

Grand Duke Constantine and his aunt, Grand Duchess Elena Pavlovna, as well as other enlightened **bureaucrats**, such as the brothers, Nicholas and Dmitri Milyutin, shared his views.

Motives for reform

Political motives

Tsarist **autocracy** depended on the **nobility**, yet many nobles who traditionally shunned business and relied on serfs to make money out of their estates were in heavy debt. A growing serf population and inadequate agricultural systems meant declining incomes and many had been forced to **mortgage** their land and even their serfs, as security for loans from the State Bank. Younger nobles had become apathetic, demotivated and critical of the regime.

Economic motives

Serfdom kept the peasants in the mirs, preventing them from moving to work in town factories and keeping the internal demand for goods low. The traditional practices of the mir prevented experimentation with new agricultural methods and rural poverty left many serfs unable to pay their taxes (the **Poll tax** and the **obruk**). Consequently, by 1859, the state faced a debt of 54 million roubles.

Moral and intellectual motives

Westernisers believed that Russia should abandon serfdom, imitating Western Europe, while **Slavophiles** favoured reforming serfdom but wanted to keep Russia's traditional peasant society. Some **intellectuals** presented the moral case against treating people like animals, whilst **nihilists** believed in sweeping away all tradition – including autocracy.

Long-term or short-term?

Below is a sample exam-style 12 mark question, which asks for a range of reasons. Understanding the difference between long-term and short-term factors helps give structure to an answer to an 'explain why' question. The chart that follows offers a list of reasons that are relevant to the answer to the question. Using the information on the opposite page and your own knowledge, decide whether each reason should be considered a long- or short-term factor and tick the appropriate box.

Explain why Alexander II embarked upon a series of reforms in Russia after 1855.

	LONG-TERM	SHORT-TERM
There was pressure from the educated classes and intellectuals to bring about change in Russia.		
The state had a 54 million rouble debt.		
Autocratic government depended on the services of the nobility, who had grown lazy and dependent on serfs.		
There was an escalation in peasant uprisings during the Crimean War.		
Nicholas and Dmitri Milyutin were enlightened bureaucrats who served Alexander II.		
Russia was economically underdeveloped.		
Russia's military incompetence had been shown during the Crimean War.		

 Identify an argument

Below are a sample exam-style 24 mark question and two sample paragraphs. One suggests a high-level answer because it advances a supported argument. The other suggests a low-level answer because it contains only description and assertion. Identify which is which. The definitions below should help you:

- **Argument**: giving a view supported by reasoning and fact
- **Assertion**: giving a view that is not supported by reasoning and fact
- **Description**: providing facts but not in support of a view.

How far was Russia's failure in the Crimean War responsible for Alexander II's interest in reform after 1855?

Paragraph 1

Although Russia entered the Crimean War in 1853, confident of victory, its hopes had rapidly been dashed in a series of disastrous military defeats. It was humiliated at the Battles of Balaclava and Inkerman in 1854 and worse still, in 1855, Russia's Black Sea naval base at Sebastopol was captured. Russia's army was reliant on peasant conscripts who served for 25 years and were subject to brutal military discipline. The commanders were poor and there was a very limited railway system. Military weapons were outdated and Russia lacked the industrial capacity to supply its troops. The huge army used up around 45 per cent of the government's annual expenditure while Russia's outdated social system maintained serfdom and there were many peasant uprisings during the Crimean War. The war was the main reason for Alexander II's interest in reform after 1855.

Paragraph 2

Russia's failures in the Crimea certainly added to Alexander II's personal concern to bring about change in Russia. He came to the throne shortly before Russia's defeat at Sebastopol in 1855 and he was acutely aware of the humiliating inadequacies the war had thrown up. Armies of serf conscripts had proved unreliable, generals incompetent, the economy unable to support the military effort and the dangers of peasant revolt were particularly frightening for an autocratic ruler. The war had also increased demands from intellectuals to tackle the outdated system of serfdom, while reformers, such as Dmitri Milyutin, with whom Alexander associated, argued for modernisation. The need to reform in order to strengthen the state and prevent a repetition of this recent disaster must have weighed heavily on Alexander II's mind in 1855.

The Emancipation of the Serfs and its impact

Revised

Procedure

The Emancipation of the Serfs was proclaimed in Alexander's Ukase of 1861. After the **Crimean War** ended in March 1856, Alexander set up committees to examine emancipation and in 1858–1859 he toured the country delivering pro-emancipation speeches. However, the provincial nobles failed to agree on measures and Alexander was exasperated by the prolonged debate which took place against a background of escalating peasant unrest. Finally, he established a commission of 38, led by Nicholas Milyutin, to produce the final measure.

This lengthy legal document, the Emancipation Ukase, only applied to the privately owned serfs. The state serfs received their freedom in 1866. It permitted some greater modernisation of the economy but its terms were not as 'liberating' in practice as its supporters had anticipated.

Terms of the Ukase	Assessment and significance
• Serfs were declared 'free' and could marry who they chose, own property, set up businesses, travel and enjoy legal rights. • Serfs were given their own cottage and an allotment of land.	• Enterprising peasants could buy up land, increase output and make money from the sale of surplus grain. • Those prepared to sell land could move to an industrialising city and obtain regular wages. • Land allocations varied; for some these were insufficient to live on. • Peasant 'rights' often remained theoretical because of the other terms of the Ukase, e.g. freedom to travel.
• Landlords were granted government bonds as compensation.	• Landowners could use compensation to redeem debts and invest in industrial enterprises. • Some could only just pay off debts and were forced to sell their remaining land.
• Serfs were required to make 49 annual 'redemption payments' for the land they were given.	• Redemption payments provoked unrest. • Land prices were sometimes fixed above market value, leaving freed serfs in considerable debt. • Some peasants had to work for their old masters or rent land from them (paid back with crops) to survive. • The 'purchasing power' of the peasants remained low; some became drifting landless labourers.
• The mir was responsible for the collection of taxes, including redemption dues. • Freed serfs had to remain within the mir until the redemption payments were complete. • The mir supervised the farming of allocated land.	• Mirs constrained the peasants, preventing them from leaving the countryside. • Mirs tended to promote restrictive and backward farming practices.
• Landowners were allowed to retain meadows, pasture, woodland and personal land. • Communal open fields were controlled by the mir for use by everyone.	• Some former serfs struggled to make a living without the use of additional land. • Serfs lost their landlords' 'protection'.
• The obruk (labour service) remained for a two-year period of 'temporary obligation'.	• Peasants were resentful; there were 647 peasant riots in four months after the decree.
• **Volosts** were established to supervise the mirs. • Volost courts, run by peasants, replaced the former landowners' jurisdiction.	• Volosts were under noble and government supervision. • Separate courts meant that peasants were treated differently from other groups.

Below are a sample exam-style 24 mark question and the outline of a paragraph written in answer to this question. The paragraph begins with a relevant comment in relation to the question and ends with a further link. However, it lacks supporting examples. Complete the paragraph by providing some factual detail in the space provided.

How successful was the Emancipation Ukase of 1861 in improving the lives of the Russian peasants?

Although the 1861 Ukase gave the freed serfs many legal freedoms, such as the right to marry whom they chose, to run businesses, own property and to travel, in many respects the Russian peasants were little better off.

_____

_____

_____

_____

Consequently, methods of farming did not significantly improve and the number of peasants able to travel to nearby towns and work in industry was limited. This restricted the opportunities the Ukase might have been expected to give the peasants in order to improve their standard of living.

Below are a sample exam-style 12 mark question and a list of reasons that could be used in the answer. Demonstrating prioritisation is one way of structuring the answer to an 'Explain why' question. Using your own knowledge and the information on the opposite page, decide the order of priority you would give to these factors. Write numbers on the spectrum below to indicate their relative importance and, beneath each, briefly justify that factor's placement, demonstrating why you feel some factors are more important than others.

Explain why many former serfs rioted against the terms of the Emancipation Edict of 1861.

1. They were required to perform labour service for two years of 'temporary obligation'.
2. They had to remain within the mir until their redemption payments had been made.
3. Landowners retained control of the meadows, pasture and woodland.
4. They had to make annual redemption payments.
5. Landlords received government bonds as compensation.
6. The mir supervised the farming of all allocated land.
7. Land prices were sometimes fixed above the market value when calculating redemption payments.
8. Landlords' protection in times of need disappeared.

Most important   Least important

Military, local government and judicial reforms

Revised

Reasons for further reform:

■ The pressure of figures such as Nicholas Milyutin and Dmitri Milyutin (Minster of War 1861–1881)

■ Disappointment at the emancipation measure on the part of peasants and landlords with continued unrest in the countryside

■ Student protests and riots in **St Petersburg**, Moscow and Kazan

■ The emancipation left issues needing resolution, e.g. conscription and control of local government and justice.

The main reforms and their success

Reforms	Assessment of success
Military reforms, 1874 • Conscription (for those over 20 years old) was made compulsory for all classes. • Length of service was reduced from 25 to 15 years, 9 years of which were spent 'in reserve' (education could reduce length of service). • **Military colonies** were abolished; welfare improvements, including the abolition of corporal punishment, were made; army service was no longer to be given as a punishment. • Military Colleges were established to train officers; promotion was by merit (rather than according to social class). • Fifteen regional commands and a new code of conduct were established. • Provision was made to modernise weaponry and build strategic railways.	• A smaller but better-trained army was created. • Costs of military to the government were reduced. • Literacy was improved through army-education campaigns. • Officers were still mainly aristocrats and the upper classes served less time, or 'bought' their way out of service. • In the war against Turkey from 1877 to 1878, victory took longer than expected; in the 1904–1905 war against the Japanese and in 1914–1917 against the Germans, Russia again suffered defeat.
Local government reforms, 1864 and 1870 • Rural councils (known as **Zemstva**) were established at district (Uezd) and provincial levels (1864) and **Dumas** were set up in the towns (1870). • Councils were to be elected through an indirect system giving an initial vote to the nobles, townspeople, Church and peasants but were weighted in favour of the nobility. • Zemstva and Dumas were given power to improve public services, including relief for the poor, and to develop industry.	Zemstva and Dumas • They offered some representative government at local level – but only spread slowly. • They were dominated by nobles and 'professionals'; peasants had limited influence. • They attracted the **liberal**-minded with local understanding and made significant improvements in welfare. • They provided a forum for debate on, and criticism of, government policies. • They had no control over local/state taxes, appointment of officials/maintenance of law and order. These remained with Tsarist-appointed provincial governors who could overturn local council decisions.
Judicial reforms, 1864 • The reforms established local courts under magistrates for minor offences; district courts with barristers, judge and jury for weightier criminal cases and the Senate for grave crimes and appeals (also Volost courts for peasant issues). • All classes were judged equal before the law and proceedings were open to the public and reporters. • Judges' training and pay were improved.	• A fairer and less corrupt system was created. • The reforms promoted legal careers – but these attracted the **intelligentsia**, who were critical of government. • The jury system could undermine government control, for example, in the case of Vera Zasulich who was acquitted of terrorism, although guilty. As a result, from 1878, political crimes were tried in special courts. • Ecclesiastical and military courts continued and the reform was not applicable to Poland.

Turning statements into reasons

Below are a sample exam-style 12 mark question and a series of statements. Read the question and turn each of the statements into a relevant reason that could be used in the answer.

Explain why military colonies were abolished in Russia in 1874.

STATEMENT	REASON
Serfdom was abolished in 1861.	
Russia lost the Crimean War of 1853–1856.	
Most Russian peasants were illiterate.	
Conscription for all over 20 became compulsory in 1874.	
Maintaining the Russian army was very expensive for the state.	
In 1874, length of service was reduced from 25 to 15 years, 9 years of which were spent 'in reserve'.	

Delete as applicable

Below are a sample exam-style 24 mark question and a paragraph written in answer to this question. Read the paragraph and decide which option (underlined) is the most appropriate. Delete the less appropriate options and complete the paragraph by justifying your selection.

How far were the military, local government and judicial reforms of 1864–1874 a result of the Emancipation of the Serfs?

The Emancipation of the Serfs was <u>the most important reason/ an important reason/ just one of many reasons</u> for the military, local government and judicial reforms of 1864–1874. Serf emancipation meant that a new system of military recruitment was needed to replace serf conscription and that the landlords' jurisdiction in the countryside had to be replaced by a new arrangement. The establishment of rural councils together with the setting up of local and volost courts <u>was in response to/ was partly in response to/ was connected with</u> the changes brought about by serf emancipation. This is because ...

_____

_____

_____

_____

Educational, cultural and economic reforms

Revised

Educational reform (1863–1864)

Broadening education at all levels of society and, in particular, improving standards of literacy and numeracy were necessary for Russia's modernisation. Despite opposition from the powerful and conservative Orthodox Church, which had traditionally dominated educational provision, the liberal-minded Minister, Alexander Golovnin, led some important changes (until 1866 when Golovnin was replaced by the conservative Tolstoy).

Changes to educational provision

- ■ The Zemstva took responsibility for primary education (replacing the Church).
- ■ Free primary education was made available to all – regardless of class and sex.
- ■ New vocational schools were set up at secondary level as an alternative to the traditional 'gymnazii' (where the curriculum was dominated by the classics).
- ■ Students from both types of secondary school could progress to university.
- ■ Universities were made self-governing in 1863 (although staff appointments had to be approved by the government). They began offering broader and more liberal courses.

Strengths of reforms	Problems with the reforms
Between 1856 and 1880: • The number of primary schools tripled. • The number of children in primary education more than doubled.	• The primary curriculum was still based on religion and offered basic reading, writing and arithmetic.
• There was a greater selection of subjects – for girls as well as boys.	• Secondary education was still fee-paying so was limited to the better-off.
• The number of students at university tripled.	• Critical students weakened the regime and the more radical joined opposition movements committed to violence.

Cultural reform (1858–1870)

- ■ A minor reform of Church organisation followed an Ecclesiastical Commission in 1862. In 1869, the system of promotion was changed to favour the capable.
- ■ Non-Russian ethnic groups were given more freedom, for example, Poles were allowed to use their own language and practise Catholicism, while laws restricting the activities of Jews were relaxed.

(Although these concessions were rescinded after the Polish revolt of 1863.) The Finns were allowed their own representative assembly.

Censorship

- ■ Control of censorship was moved from the conservative Orthodox Church to the government which could prevent publication and fine publishers, but the latter could appeal through the courts.
- ■ New regulations in 1865 reduced restrictions on newspapers and books to allow comment on government policy in editorials and the publication of foreign works.

Strengths of reforms	Problems with the reforms
• There was a tenfold increase in the number of books published in the years 1859–1894.	• Censorship continued. • More criticisms of the government appeared.

Economic reform (1860–1878)

Since Russia did not possess a wealthy middle class, Mikhail von Reutern (Minister of Finance 1862–1878) believed the government must direct economic change.

Details of economic reforms

- • Tax-farming was abolished (companies could no longer buy the right to collect taxes).
- • The treasury was reformed and budgeting and auditing systems were established.
- • Credit facilities were made available through the establishment of banks.
- • Subsidies were offered to private railway companies and other industrial initiatives.
- • Government-guaranteed annual dividends were provided for foreign investors.
- • Tariffs on trade were lowered and trade treaties were negotiated.

Strengths of reforms	Limitations of reforms
• The cotton industry expanded and mining grew in the Donets coalfield. • There was some improvement in agriculture.	• Transport and labour mobility remained limited. • Growth was slow. • The tax system was not changed and kept the peasants poor. • The Russian currency was unstable and much income went towards paying off debts.

Eliminate irrelevance

Below are a sample exam-style 24 mark question and a paragraph written in answer to it. Read the paragraph and identify parts that are not directly relevant or helpful to the question. Draw a line through the information that is irrelevant and justify your deletions in the margin.

How far did the reforms of Alexander II transform Russian society between 1861 and 1881?

Among the reforms that transformed Russian society were changes in education. The changes were introduced by Alexander II's Education Minister, Golovnin, who, like the Milyutin brothers, had liberal ideas. The educational changes came to an end when Golovnin was replaced by the conservative Tolstoy in 1866. In 1864, the new Zemstva were given responsibility for the provision of education in their own areas. These Zemstva were elected councils chosen by the nobles, townspeople, Church and peasants, although voting was arranged in a way that allowed the nobles more influence. The schools they established were made available to all, regardless of sex or background, which helped transform society, even though the poor rarely got beyond primary level. Although the serfs had been emancipated in 1861, many were still very poor and reliant on subsistence farming. The educational curriculum was also expanded with new scientific subjects and vocational secondary schools offering opportunities for advancement. There was still a very small middle class in Russia though. The universities were made self-governing which gave them more control over appointments and the courses they offered. This transformed society by creating a new group of critical and radical students.

Develop the detail

Below are a sample exam-style 24 mark question and a paragraph written in answer to this. The paragraph contains a limited amount of detail. Annotate the paragraph to add additional detail to the answer.

How successful were Alexander II's reforms in turning Russia into a 'modern' state?

Alexander II's economic reforms went some way towards making Russia a 'modern' state. The government took responsibility for the development of industry and encouraged investment. Despite all this, capital expansion was still slow, however. Despite all the encouragement, Russia was still predominantly rural and undeveloped at the time of Alexander's death in 1881.

Alexander and reaction

A period of **reaction** set in, in the late 1860s for the following reasons:

- A revolt in Poland in 1863
- The death of Alexander's eldest son and heir in 1865
- Alexander's new mistress, Caterina Dolgoruki, who distanced him from his liberal relatives
- An assassination attempt in 1866.

Alexander appointed reactionary ministers, such as Dmitri Tolstoy, Pyotr Shuvalov, Alexander Timashev and Konstantin Pahlen, who argued that westernising changes were weakening Russia. So, although military and economic reforms continued, Alexander's other reforming impulses were halted, or even reversed.

Area	Policies	Results
Education	• Authority over primary schools was returned to the Church and the activities of the Zemstva were restricted. • The gymnazii were ordered to remove from the curriculum the sciences they had introduced. • Students from vocational schools could only go to higher technical institutions (1871), not university. • Subjects thought to encourage critical thought, such as literature and history, were banned in universities. • Student organisations were banned. • University appointments could be vetoed by the government.	• Religious control was reasserted. • The curriculum was restricted. • Female education declined. • Many students escaped restrictions by studying abroad.
Police and the law courts	• The work of the **Third Section** (secret police) was increased. • Until 1878 political offenders could face **show trials**. • 1878: political crimes were tried in secret in military courts. • 1879: governor-generals were given emergency powers to use military courts and impose exile.	• Critics and opponents thrived underground. • The 'show trials' were abandoned after sympathetic juries acquitted the accused, for example Vera Zasulich (see page 8).
Cultural reform	• Poles lost their liberties after the revolt in 1863. • Russian culture was enforced on the **national minorities** (beginning '**Russification**'). • Censorship was tightened.	• There was hostility towards non-Russians. • New opposition movements emerged.

A change of heart?

The **Russo-Turkish War** (1877–1878), famine (1879–1880), the beginnings of an industrial recession and further assassination attempts in 1879 and 1880 led Alexander II to establish a commission under Count Loris-Melikov who had been appointed Minister of the Interior in 1880 to investigate the spread of revolutionary activity. This led to the:

- release of political prisoners
- relaxation of censorship
- lifting of restrictions on the activities of the Zemstva
- removal of the **salt tax**
- abolition of the Third Section (replaced by the **Okhrana**).

Loris-Melikov subsequently produced the Loris-Melikov Constitution, which proposed that elected representatives from the nobility, Zemstva and town dumas should form a National Duma to discuss (although not propose or veto) some state decrees. Alexander was in approval, and was about to meet a council of ministers to discuss this when he was killed by a bomb in March 1881.

Creating a Venn diagram

Below is a sample exam-style 12 mark question. Use your own knowledge and the information on the opposite page to produce a Venn diagram plan for an answer to this question which groups the reasons thematically.

Explain why Alexander II's policies became more reactionary after 1866.

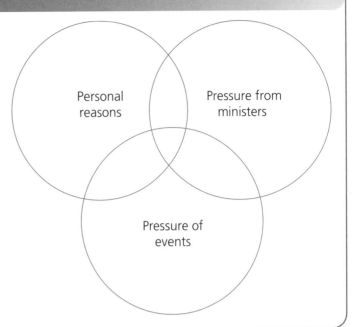

Personal reasons

Pressure from ministers

Pressure of events

You're the examiner

Below are a sample exam-style 24 mark question and a paragraph written in answer to this question. Read the paragraph, and the mark scheme provided on page 3. Decide which level you would award the paragraph. Write the level below, along with a justification for your decision.

How successful was Alexander II in reforming Russia between 1855 and 1881?

After 1866, when a student tried to assassinate the Tsar, there were no more reforms in Russia. This was mostly because of Tolstoy, Alexander's new reactionary minister of education. He put schools back in the hands of the Church again and would not allow the universities any freedom. Children had to recite religious passages and learn how to behave. It was not an education. As well as this, censorship became strong again so that people couldn't read what they wanted and publishers could not print anything that was at all critical. It seemed as though all the good work that Alexander had tried to do in his first years as Tsar was undone. The secret police were also kept busy. They had to chase and destroy all opposition which usually meant that opponents were forced into exile. This was the opposite of reform. Alexander even tried to make an example of opponents in show trials which ordinary people could watch. They didn't work though, because the juries were more inclined to support the radicals and so they found them 'not-guilty', which was humiliating for the Tsar and his ministers. Secret military courts were used for trials and all the previous reforms came to an end. Alexander seemed to have given up trying. He was too busy with his new mistress to care and he let his ministers do as they wished.

Level: Reason for choosing this level:

_____

_____

_____

The emergence of opposition to the Tsarist regime

Revised

The spread of opposition

Alexander's reforms stimulated both excitement and disappointment, leading to the growth of opposition groups.

- The relaxation of the censorship laws encouraged the spread of more radical journals and books whilst the educational changes brought a larger and more independent student population keen to see their country modernise and throw off its 'backward' image.

- Local government changes also gave middle-class intellectuals a platform on which to debate their views about the future of Russia, whilst the expansion of the court system offered opportunities for keen young lawyers to air their ideas.

- The more repressive atmosphere after 1866 helped reinforce the belief in change, although demands ranged from fairly moderate liberal ideas to more extreme pressure for a complete change in society (socialism).

Radical thinkers

Radical thinkers whose works began to influence the young and educated Russians to adopt **socialist** ideas included:

- **Nikolai Chernyshevsky**, author of a radical journal, 'The Contemporary' and book, *What Is To Be Done?* (1863) both of which spread the view that the peasants had to be made leaders of revolutionary change.

- **Alexander Herzen**, editor of the journal, 'The Bell', which also advocated a new peasant-based social structure.

- **Mikhail Bakunin**, an anarchist and socialist who suggested private ownership of land should be replaced by collective ownership and that income should be based on the number of hours worked. In 1869, he wrote the book, *Catechism of a Revolutionary* together with **Sergei Nechaev**. Published in Switzerland and secretly smuggled into Russia, this encouraged opponents of Tsardom to be merciless in the pursuit of revolutionary change.

- Bakunin also translated Karl Marx's *Communist Manifesto* into Russian in 1869; and the first volume of Marx's *Das Kapital* was published in Russia in 1872. Karl Marx was a German philosopher whose theories about economics, society and politics were based on the idea that society had evolved through a series of class struggles and that a final struggle between an industrial working class (proletariat) and capitalist middle class (bourgeoisie) would herald, after a short 'dictatorship of the proletariat', a perfect society in which all would be equal.

Emergence of new opposition groups

Underground reading circles and societies spread these new intellectual ideas and new groups began to emerge:

- 1862: Establishment of Young Russia, a student organisation hostile to both the Tsar and the Church. This was probably behind a series of fires in St Petersburg which destroyed over 2000 shops in 1862.

- 1863: 'The Organisation' – this was set up by students at Moscow University to co-ordinate student revolutionary activities.

- 1864: The St Petersburg Zemstvo demanded a central body to organise regional Zemstva. This was a fairly mild liberal demand but heralded the first step towards demands for a national parliament.

- c. 1869–1872 **Populism** emerged, inspired by Sergei Nechaev and **Pyotr Lavrov**, as young people set out to persuade the peasantry about their socialist ideas.

Spider diagram

Below are a sample exam-style 12 mark question and the beginnings of a spider diagram to identify relevant reasons. Read the question and complete the spider diagram with a sentence of explanation. Then prioritise your reasons by adding numbers to each oval – with 1 as the most important reason and 6 as the least important.

Explain why there was a growth in opposition to the Tsarist regime during the reign of Alexander II.

Turning assertion into argument

Below are a sample exam-style 24 mark question and a series of assertions. Read the question and then add a justification to each of the assertions to turn it into a supported view, so creating an argument.

How far was the growth of opposition to the Tsarist regime the result of the Tsar's own reforms?

The growth of opposition was the result of Alexander II's judicial reforms.

_____

_____

The growth of opposition came about because Alexander II relaxed censorship.

_____

_____

The growth of opposition was the result of Alexander's reform of education and the universities.

_____

_____

Populism and radical opposition

The spread of opposition 1870–1881

- Between 1869 and 1872, Sergei Nechaev's 'Chaikovsky Circle' smuggled books into Russia encouraging the Populist ideas of land redistribution and fairer taxes.

- 1874: Pyotr Lavrov encouraged c. 2000 young people, mainly students, to 'go to the people'. These **Narodniks** (Populists) tried to dress and talk like peasants to gain acceptance in villages and spread their ideas. However, ignorance, loyalty to the Church and to the Tsar and fear that the Narodniks were secret police agents led peasants to reject them and sometimes hand them over to the police. There were 1600 arrests.

- 1876: a Second Narodnik movement was attempted but, like the first, it failed with many arrests.

- 1877: the remaining Narodniks established **Land and Liberty** with similar aims but a commitment to assassination. Their efforts included:

  – the assassination of General Mezemstev, head of the secret police, 1878

  – the assassination of Prince Krapotkin, Governor-General of Kharkoff, 1879

  – several attempts on the Tsar's life.

- In 1879, Land and Liberty split into:

The Black Partition	The People's Will
• Organised by Georgi Plekhanov • Aimed to 'partition the **black soil**' provinces among the peasants • Worked peacefully among peasants • Spread radical materials among students and workers • Weakened by arrests in 1880 to 1881 and broke up • Plekhanov and other leaders subsequently created the first Russian Marxist association – the Emancipation of Labour – in Geneva, 1883.	• Led by Timofei Mikhailov • Aimed to establish representative government and land redistribution • Larger than the Black Partition • Advocated violent methods and assassination (particularly of the Tsar) • March 1881 – succeeded in assassinating Alexander II with a bomb as he was travelling by coach to the **Winter Palace** in St Petersburg.

Significance of the spread of opposition

- Government failures (e.g. the show trials) and assassinations helped suggest the Tsarist regime lacked authority.

- Demands for 'reform from below' had grown and spread socially and geographically.

- Opposition ranged from the moderate liberal intelligentsia, particularly Zemstva members, to the People's Will extremists. The Zemstva engaged in talks with Land and Liberty although they disapproved of assassinations.

- The conservative bureaucracy, nobles and landowners who had opposed Alexander's reforms forced him to adopt a more reactionary stance by linking reform to growing opposition.

Make the links

Below are a sample exam-style 12 mark question and a series of relevant reasons that could be used in the answer. Read the question and add a comment and linking phrase to each reason to explain each reason and show how it relates to the following one.

Explain why the Narodnik movement was a failure in the 1870s.

Reason	Comment and linking phrase leading to the next reason
The Narodniks were mostly upper-class students	
The peasants did not understand the Narodniks	
Peasants turned the Narodniks over to the authorities.	

How important?

Below is a sample exam-style 24 mark question which asks you about the importance of a factor. Questions like this can be answered by balancing the way the factor was important against the ways in which it was not. A series of statements relevant to the question is given below. Using your own knowledge and the information on the previous pages, decide whether these statements suggest the factor was important or not important and tick the appropriate box.

How important were opposition groups in undermining the Tsarist regime by 1881?

	IMPORTANT	NOT IMPORTANT
Young Russia was probably behind a series of fires in St Petersburg in 1862.		
Socialist writings had a minority readership – mostly students and the liberal intelligentsia.		
The St Petersburg Zemstvo demanded a central body to organise regional Zemstva.		
Marxism was discussed in underground reading circles.		
Peasants were suspicious of the Narodniks and sometimes reported them to the police.		
The head of the Third Section was assassinated.		
Land and Liberty held discussions with the Zemstva.		
Many members of the Black Partition were arrested from 1880 to 1881.		
The People's Will assassinated Alexander II in March 1881.		

Exam focus

Below is a sample A grade answer for a 12 mark question. Read the answer, the brief plan and the examiner's comments around it.

Explain why Tsar Alexander II was assassinated in 1881.

The plan identifies three factors.

Plan:

- People's Will committed to assassination

- Frustration at Tsar's failure to follow through reforming impulses

- Spread of discontent, encouraged by early reforms/hopes

There is direct reference to what the question asks. This is a very good way to begin an answer.

Tsar Alexander II was assassinated on 1 March 1881 because a radical member of the People's Will found himself in an ideal position from which to throw a bomb directly at the Tsar. This opportunity arose as the Tsar inspected the damage inflicted by a previous bomb which had landed among the Cossacks accompanying his carriage on its way to the Winter Palace. The People's Will, which had emerged from the Land and Liberty organisation in 1879, and derived from the Populist tradition, was committed to changing the political and social structure of Russia and believed the only way to do this was to employ violent methods. It had committed itself to the assassination of the Tsar (if no new constitution was granted) in 1879 and it had already attempted to carry out this threat several times by 1881.

This paragraph gives an immediate and specific reason for the assassination and explains the event with reference to the assassin and his organisation.

The People's Will's commitment to assassination only came about, however, because of the frustration of its members with the Tsar's failure to carry through widescale and far-reaching reform. Above all, they sought a redistribution of land, giving land to the peasantry and, to facilitate this, a representative government in place of the autocracy. Alexander II had adamantly refused to go as far as this, and although he had ultimately given his tentative approval to a document drawn up by Loris-Melikov in 1881, which would have allowed elected representatives of the Zemstva, nobility and town governments to have had some say in the discussion of state decrees, even if this had become law, it fell far short of what the People's Will wanted.

Here is an excellent link to a different reason – the need for reform.

Again there is a clear link to the third reason and the answer develops with some very precise examples, with dates given.

Moreover, the People's Will's frustrations were all the more acute because of the hopes engendered by Alexander II's early reforming impulses, particularly the Emancipation of the Serfs (1861) and the creation of the Zemstva (1864). These, coupled with a relaxation of censorship and a more liberal University system, produced the very students who were attracted to organisations such as the People's Will.

The early reforms had encouraged the Populists and other radical opponents to believe that major reform might soon be granted 'from above', but they were to be bitterly disappointed, particularly when Alexander grew more repressive after 1866. In the later years of Alexander's reign, the police forces were strengthened and the activities of the Third Section stepped up. The Populist attempts to 'go to the people' and rouse peasant discontent in 1874 and 1876 had failed miserably and, consequently, the assassination of the Tsar seemed the only way forward.

Alexander II was therefore assassinated in 1881 because he had raised hopes which, being too rooted in his belief in his God-given autocracy, he had failed to fulfil and which had given both fuel and opportunity to radical revolutionaries who had a clear programme for change and a commitment to violent action in order to achieve that change. The assassination itself was the result of a 'lucky' break after a series of earlier failures. It was no random event, but the result of a good number of underlying issues and frustrations.

The conclusion summarises the three reasons and emphasises how they interlink.

12/12

This answer offers three different and well-linked reasons. It is impressive because of the amount of precise and accurate detail it conveys and the structured way in which the factors are presented. It shows a very high level of understanding and so gains full marks.

Identifying links in a 12 mark answer

This response shows a high-level answer to an 'explain why' question which reaches the top mark because it contains some impressive links between the factors it advances. Go through the answer and make a list of those links. Consider how these links are incorporated into the answer.

Section 2:
Political reaction: social and economic change, 1881–1904

Industrialisation: the work of Vyshnegradsky and Witte

Revised

State capitalism

Despite some progress under Reutern (see page 10), Russia still remained undeveloped in relation to western Europe. Under Alexander III (1881–1894) and Nicholas II (1894–1917), ministers expanded the programme of 'state capitalism'.

Ivan Vyshnegradsky (Finance Minister, 1887–1892)

Vyshnegradsky tried to build up state capital by increasing:

- **indirect taxation**
- **import tariffs** (the 1891 Tariff Act set import duties at 33 per cent)
- grain exports by forcing **peasants** to sell grain to the state
- loans from abroad (e.g. from France, 1888).

Results

- Grain exports increased by 18 per cent (1881–1891) and by 1892 the budget was in surplus.
- Peasants suffered from heavy taxation, high goods prices and grain requisitions.
- A famine (1891–1892) following a bad harvest killed c. 350,000 people and Vyshnegradsky was dismissed.

Sergei Witte (Finance Minister, 1892–1903)

Witte believed industrialisation was essential to curb revolutionary unrest. Consequently the drive for growth continued.

Encouraging industrial development

- **Interest rates** were raised to encourage foreign loans.
- A new rouble, backed by gold, was issued in 1897 to increase business confidence.
- Foreign experts (engineers and managers) and skilled foreign workers were brought in.
- The government invested in railways.
- Heavy industry was prioritised over lighter industry and large factory units of over 1000 workers were built to maximise production.

- Peasants were encouraged to relocate. The development of the **Trans-Siberian railway** and an 1896 government scheme promoted resettlement in Siberia where there were new farming opportunities and no history of **serfdom**.

Results

- The cost to the government was high and Russia became dependent on foreign investment which increased nearly tenfold 1880–1900.
- The promise of regular wages lured more peasants into industrial centres, although some still returned to their villages at harvest time.
- The number of factory workers doubled 1887–1908 but only 750,000 peasants, (from a peasant population of nearly 97 million) moved to Siberia.
- Although most overseas trade was still carried in foreign ships and roads remained poor, the growth of long-distance railway lines opened up the interior, enabled raw materials to travel to industrial plants and linked agricultural areas to industrial cities and ports.
- Railway development stimulated heavy steel industries, reduced transport costs for manufacturers and provided government revenue.
- By 1897 Russia was the fourth largest industrialised economy. Industry was growing at more than 8 per cent per year (1894–1904), surpassing other industrial countries, although grain remained Russia's largest export.
- The coal/iron industries of the Donbas region in the Ukraine and the oil fields of Baku (on the Caspian Sea) boomed with the help of foreign investors such as the Nobel, Rothschild and Vishau families. More than half the world's oil came from Baku by 1901.

	1880	1890	1900	1910
Coal	3.2	5.9	16.1	25.4
Pig iron	0.42	0.89	2.66	3.0
Crude oil	0.5	3.9	10.2	12.1

Production in millions of metric tons

Prioritisation

Below are a sample exam-style 12 mark question and a list of reasons that could be used in the answer. Demonstrating prioritisation is one way of structuring the answer to an 'Explain why' question. Using your own knowledge and the information on the opposite page, decide the order of priority you would give to these factors. Write numbers on the spectrum below to indicate their relative importance and, beneath each, briefly justify that factor's placement, demonstrating why you feel some factors are more important than others.

Explain why the Russian state promoted the growth of the railway system in the 1890s.

1. To stimulate other industries
2. To reduce prices of goods
3. To act in place of a Russian middle class
4. To provide jobs
5. To open up less accessible areas
6. To provide an infrastructure
7. To obtain revenue
8. To stimulate agriculture

Most important   Least important

Identify an argument

Below are a sample exam-style 24 mark question and two sample paragraphs. One suggests a high-level answer because it advances a supported argument. The other suggests a low-level answer because it contains only description and assertion. Identify which is which. The definitions below should help you:

- **Argument**: giving a view supported by reasoning and fact
- **Assertion**: giving a view that is not supported by reasoning and fact
- **Description**: providing facts but not in support of a view.

How important was an increase in grain exports for the industrialisation of Russia between 1881 and 1904?

Paragraph 1

Ivan Vyshnegradsky became finance minister in 1887 and set out to modernise the Russian economy in order to help Russia catch up with the West and become an industrial nation. He increased grain exports by taking more grain from the peasants. This was a harsh policy which led to a famine in 1891–1892, killing peasants who had been forced to sell their grain to the state and had no reserves when they faced a poor harvest. However, grain exports grew by 18 per cent to 1891. This meant Vyshnegradsky had more money for industrialisation and although he was dismissed in 1892 for helping bring about the famine, his policies were continued by the next finance minister, Sergei Witte.

Paragraph 2

Increasing grain exports was very important in providing the government with the necessary capital with which to promote Russian industrialisation. Since grain was the only commodity that Russia had in sufficient abundance to export, it is hardly surprising that both Vyshnegradsky and Witte squeezed the peasants hard so as to be able to sell more abroad. Without the capital grain exports created, the government would not have been in a position to sponsor the railways and the large factories that revolutionised Russia's coal, iron and oil industries, and government sponsorship was vital for industrialisation since there was no capitalist middle class in Russia to fulfil this role. Although the government could raise money by taking out foreign loans, this was a far less satisfactory means of capital accumulation than expanding grain exports, since loans had to be paid back with interest.

The social impact of industrial change

Whilst industrialisation helped to strengthen the Russian economy, it also brought a number of changes, some of which were to prove detrimental to the **Tsarist** regime. A new middle class and urban working class emerged.

The middle class

White-collar workers, including factory and workshop owners, managers, experts, traders and professionals (such as bankers and teachers) became more prominent in society and many played a major role in the **Zemstva** and **Dumas**. However, the lack of a national parliament often made them oppositional, rather than (as in western democracies) 'pillars of the establishment'.

Urban growth and conditions

The urban population quadrupled from 7 to 28 million between 1867 and 1917 and by 1900, factory workers made up three per cent of the population. However, most suffered appalling working and living conditions and mortality rates were high. Some rented rooms in overcrowded blocks while others were housed in barrack-style factory accommodation where they ate in communal canteens and shared bath-houses. The least fortunate slept alongside their machines in the factories. Around 40 per cent of rented houses in **St Petersburg** had no running water and sewage was collected by handcarts.

There was limited regulation in the workplace, allowing employers to pay minimal wages which failed to keep pace with inflation. Women, who comprised a fifth of the workforce by 1914, were the lowest paid and an industrial depression from 1900 to 1908 hit workers hard. Unions and strikes were officially banned before 1905, although some took place illegally and were usually violently suppressed.

There was some improvement in the provision of education and in social welfare before 1914, as seen below, but every change led to demands for more.

Date	Law
1885	Night-time work for children and women was banned.
1886	Contracts of employment had to be drawn up.
1892	Female labour was banned in mines and employment of children under twelve was banned.
1897	Working hours were reduced to 11.5 per day.
1903	Factory inspectorate was expanded.
1912	Health insurance was introduced.

Peasants

Agricultural improvements were neglected in the drive for industrialisation and many peasants lived at subsistence level, subject to recurrent famine (e.g. 1891–1892, 1898 and 1901). Grain output per acre was less than a third of that of Britain, Germany or the USA yet peasants were driven hard to produce a surplus for export and pay high taxes. Rural population growth made conditions worse, particularly as holdings were divided between sons and the amount of land farmed by individual families declined. The establishment of the Nobles' and Peasants' Land Banks (1882 and 1885) to provide loans for the purchase of more land helped increase peasant ownership but left some landless and others in huge debt. (Landowners also struggled to meet debts and around a third of their land was sold to townsmen or peasants from 1861 to 1905.)

Consequently, the gulf between the richer (**kulak**) peasants – who could afford to employ labour – and the poorest, landless peasants widened and too few moved to the towns to ease the pressure of resources. Peasant mortality rates were high and large numbers were considered unfit for military service. Average life expectancy in 1900 was 27.25 for males and 29.83 for females (in England the joint average was 45.25).

Complete the paragraph

Below are a sample exam-style 24 mark question and the outline of a paragraph written in answer to this question. The paragraph begins with a relevant comment in relation to the question and ends with a further link. However, it lacks supporting examples. Complete the paragraph by providing some factual detail in the space provided.

How far did the economic changes of the years 1881–1905 benefit the urban working class in Russia?

Although the economic changes of the years 1881–1905 brought some benefits for the urban working class in terms of regular employment and wages, overall the working classes in the industrial towns and cities suffered more than they benefited. For example ...

_____

_____

_____

_____

_____

Consequently, although increased industrialisation was ultimately to raise standards of living in Russia, in these early years of industrialisation, the working classes saw few of the rewards of economic change.

Turning statements into reasons

Below are a sample exam-style 12 mark question and a series of statements. Read the question and turn each of the statements into a relevant reason that could be used in the answer.

Explain why peasants had a low standard of living in the 1890s.

STATEMENT	REASON
Russia's population had doubled in the second half of the nineteenth century.	
Peasants lived in mirs, which collected their redemption payments.	
The government was committed to the promotion of industrialisation.	
Kulaks could afford to employ labour.	
Former state peasants were granted more land than the former privately owned serfs.	
Peasant land banks were introduced in 1885.	
America was able to export cheap grain to Europe.	

The growth of opposition

Liberal intelligentsia

Industrial and educational expansion produced a middle class seeking **liberal** change.

Zemstva

The professionals elected to the Zemstva (often experts in education, health or law) were highly critical of **autocracy**. Alexander III's introduction of **Land Captains** in 1889 to remove complaining Zemstva members and overrule Zemstva decisions only increased their opposition. Furthermore, the government's inability to co-ordinate famine relief (1891–1892), which the Zemstva were left to provide, exemplified Tsarist incompetence. However, when the Zemstvo of Tver petitioned Nicholas II for a National Duma (parliament) in 1895, this was dismissed as a 'senseless dream'. An attempt to create an All-Zemstva organisation (1896) was also banned.

Frustrated liberals formed 'Beseda', the first organised liberal opposition group in 1899. This merged with the Union of Liberation, founded by Pyotr Struve, in 1903. Struve was a moderate Marxist who believed in constitutional government. Fifty society banquets were held over the winter of 1904 to spread the Union's message.

Other liberal critics

Liberal **intellectuals**, such as the author Leo Tolstoy, helped popularise the need for political change. Even S. V. Zubatov, the head of the Moscow **Okhrana** favoured liberalisation and was given permission to legalise **trade unions** in 1900. His experiment was abandoned in 1903 when one union attempted a general strike.

Radical opposition

Despite his repressive action (see page 26), Alexander III failed to eradicate radical opposition.

- Students reformed the People's Will in 1886. In 1887, five members, including Lenin's brother (Alexander Ulyanov), were executed for plotting the assassination of Alexander III.
- **Populism** (see page 16) re-emerged in the universities in 1899. In 1901, the Minister of Education, Bogolepov, was assassinated.

The Socialist Revolutionary Party (SR)

The **Socialist Revolutionary Party** was established in 1901. It combined **Marxism** with the Populist belief in land redistribution. Viktor Chernov edited the party journal 'Revolutionary Russia' and exhorted both peasantry and urban workers to challenge autocracy. The SRs carried out 2000 political assassinations, from 1901 to 1905, including Spyagin and von Plehve.

The Social Democratic Party (SD)

Plekhanov (see page 16) established the first Russian Marxist association, the **Emancipation** of Labour, in 1883, in Geneva. It smuggled Marxist literature, including Plekhanov's *Socialism and the Political Struggle* (1883) into Russia encouraging workers to work with the bourgeoisie to overthrow Tsardom. Plekhanov believed attempts to rouse the peasantry were futile. Marxism attracted an educated following, including Vladimir Ulyanov – known as Lenin from 1901. Lenin was attracted to Marxism when he was a St Petersburg law student. He met Plekhanov on a tour of Europe in 1895, but was arrested and exiled to Siberia until 1900.

The **Social Democratic Workers' Party** was founded at a congress in Minsk in 1898. Only nine delegates attended, but they wrote a manifesto and elected a three-man Central Committee, two of whom were immediately arrested. From exile in Switzerland, Lenin wrote for the party newspaper, 'The Spark' (Iskra) from 1902 and produced a pamphlet, 'What is to be done?'. In 1903, 51 delegates attended the second congress in Brussels, then London, but disagreements between Lenin and Martov, the co-editor of Iskra, split ranks. Lenin's followers became known as **Bolsheviks** after winning a crucial vote, while Martov's followers were called **Mensheviks**. Their differences can be seen below:

Lenin's followers wanted a small, centrally controlled, highly disciplined party of professional revolutionaries who would lead the revolution on behalf of the workers. They refused to work with other parties and trade unions and believed the bourgeois and proletarian revolutions could occur simultaneously.

Martov's followers wanted a democratic party, that was open to all, and was willing to co-operate with other parties and unions. They believed that the workers should lead the revolution and that a proletarian revolution could only happen after the bourgeois revolution.

Below are a sample exam-style 24 mark question and a paragraph written in answer to this question. Read the paragraph and decide which option (underlined) is the most appropriate. Delete the less appropriate options and complete the paragraph by justifying your selection.

How far were the demands of opposition movements a threat to the Tsarist governments in the years 1881–1904?

The demands of opposition movements were <u>a major threat/ a fairly important threat/ not a particularly major threat</u> to the Tsarist governments in the years 1881–1904. The Liberal intelligentsia's desire for a national Duma was <u>very threatening/ quite threatening/ not particularly threatening</u> to the Tsarist autocracy while the aims of the Radical Opposition which was divided between the Socialist Revolutionaries and Social Democrats was <u>very threatening/ quite threatening/ not particularly threatening</u>. This was because....

_____

_____

_____

_____

_____

Below is a sample exam-style 12 mark question, which asks for a range of reasons. Understanding the difference between long-term and short-term factors helps give structure to an answer to an 'explain why' question. The chart that follows offers a list of reasons that are relevant to the answer to the question. Using the information on the opposite page and your own knowledge, decide whether each reason should be considered a long- or short-term factor and tick the appropriate box.

Explain why the Bolshevik Party was established in 1903.

	LONG-TERM	SHORT-TERM
Martov wanted to co-operate with other liberal parties, trade unions and co-operatives.		
Plekhanov created The Emancipation of Labour – a Marxist association.		
Lenin was a very ambitious and committed Marxist who believed he knew what was best for the party.		
Lenin wrote 'What is to be done?', emphasising the importance of workers' revolution over trade unionism.		
Lenin's brother was hanged after involvement in a plot to assassinate Alexander III.		
The Social Democratic Party's first congress was broken up and its leaders were arrested.		
Marxism was able to spread through literature that was smuggled into Russia.		
Lenin wanted a highly disciplined party of professional revolutionaries to lead the proletariat.		

The rule of Tsars Alexander III and Nicholas II to 1904

The reassertion of autocracy

- Both Alexander III and Nicholas II were advised by the **reactionary** Konstantin Pobedonostev, procurator of the Holy Synod. He encouraged them to reassert the principle of autocracy and uphold Orthodoxy and 'Nationalism', which effectively meant **Russification** – the enforcing of Russian language on the culture of the other ethnic peoples of the Empire.

- Alexander III arrested 150 members of the People's Will and publicly hanged those responsible for his father's assassination and increased the powers of the police. He made the Department of Police (which supervised the **Gendarmerie** and Okhrana (secret police)) responsible to the Ministry of Internal Affairs so that its activities could be monitored. Spies and counter-spies were also widely used.

- From 1881 the government encouraged anti-Jewish **pogroms**. Other ethnic groups were also victimised.

- From 1882, any area of the Empire could be deemed an 'area of subversion' with police agents able to arrest, imprison or exile on suspicion.

- In 1885, closed court sessions (where trials were held in secret) without juries were reintroduced.

- In 1889, Alexander III introduced Land Captains, appointed from the **nobility**. These replaced local magistrates and had the power to over-ride Zemstva elections and decisions. They could overturn the judgements of local courts and order the flogging of peasants.

- In 1890, the peasant vote to the Zemstva was reduced (and similar measures made it difficult for the less wealthy to vote for town Dumas in 1892).

- In 1900, there was a purge of outspoken liberal members in the Zemstva.

The personal rule of Nicholas II

Tsar Nicholas II (1894–1917), who had been brought up to fear but respect his powerful **autocratic** father, was ill-suited to become Tsar. He was naturally reserved and although a hard-working cultured individual who could speak several languages, he was not interested in politics. He readily admitted he had little idea of how to rule when he first came to the throne. Nevertheless, he felt he had a God-given duty to fulfil and the weight of this responsibility affected him greatly. He was determined to rule 'as his father had done', yet he proved incapable of making firm decisions and providing any sense of direction. He tried to deal with disquiet by stepping up surveillance and relying on the army and martial law. He maintained his father's policy of extending Church influence over education, discriminating against those of lowly background, barring women from universities and making university appointments dependent on the political reliability of the candidate. Student demonstrations were brutally crushed and, in 1901, 13 young people were killed by a **Cossack** charge in St Petersburg and 1500 more were imprisoned.

The situation by 1904

There was widespread unrest in both towns and the countryside as the Tsarist government appeared to offer no prospect of change and the Tsar, who was easily influenced, had dismissed his most competent adviser, Sergei Witte (see page 20) in 1903, leaving himself surrounded by reactionary ministers.

There were many incidents of arson in the countryside during the turbulent 'years of the Red Cockerel' (1903–1904) which were so called because the leaping flames resembled a Cock's comb. While peasants suffering from land-hunger destroyed landlords' barns and seized woodland and pasture, industrial workers formed illegal trade unions and became involved in strikes. The experiment with legalised trade unions under Zubatov in Moscow (see page 24) failed, but in St Petersburg **Father Gapon** set up a union along similar lines in 1904 (and won the approval of Plehve, the Minister for Internal Affairs). This union was to prove far more significant than anyone had foreseen.

Below are a sample exam-style 24 mark question and a paragraph written in answer to it. Read the paragraph and identify parts that are not directly relevant or helpful to the question. Draw a line through the information that is irrelevant and justify your deletions in the margin.

How successful were Alexander III and Nicholas II in upholding the principle of autocracy in the years 1881 to 1904?

Both Alexander III and Nicholas II tried to uphold the principle of autocracy and, for the most part, they were successful until 1904. Alexander III arrested 150 members of the People's Will and hanged those responsible for his father's murder at the beginning of his reign. Censorship and security were tightened and the Tsar withdrew to his fortified castle at Gatchina in case there were further assassination attempts. Alexander increased the powers of the police and used both gendarmes, recruited from the nobility, and the secret forces of the Okhrana to prevent opposition. During Alexander II's reign, the Populist Opposition Movement had emerged and then developed into Land and Liberty. In 1879, this had split into the two factions — the Black Partition and the People's Will. From 1882, any area of the Empire could be considered an 'area of subversion' and the police could arrest, imprison and exile at will. In 1901, in Nicholas' reign, a group of mounted Cossacks charged a student demonstration, killing 13, while 1500 students were imprisoned. Both tsars were advised by Pobedonostev who had highly reactionary views. Alexander III appointed Land Captains from noble families in 1889. They partially replaced the local magistrates and Zemstva, which were considered too liberal. Peasant and liberal representation on the Zemstva was reduced, some trials were again held in secret and Nicholas openly admitted that politics bored him.

Below is a sample exam-style 12 mark question. Use your own knowledge and the information on the opposite page to produce a Venn diagram plan for an answer to this question which groups the reasons thematically.

Explain why there was so much unrest in Russia in the years 1903–1904.

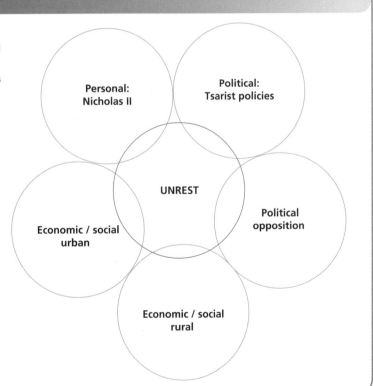

Exam focus

Below is a sample A grade essay for a 24 mark question. Read the essay and the examiner's comments around it.

How successful were the Tsarist governments in promoting economic modernisation in the years 1861–1905?

> This directly focused opening sentence offers one side of the picture.

In many respects, the Tsarist governments appear to have been extremely successful in promoting economic modernisation. Before 1861, Russia was among the most backward nations of Europe, both industrially and agriculturally, and was the last to retain a serf economy; by 1905, it was the fourth largest industrial economy and its agriculture was being transformed as more wealthy kulak-peasants were buying out the less successful former serfs and improving the land they farmed. The transformation in a short space of time certainly appeared impressive. Between 1894 and 1904, Russia's annual rate of growth was, at 8 per cent, higher than that of any other industrial country. Nevertheless, the statistics hide major problems within the economy and, in reality, economic modernisation had not been successfully achieved in Russia by 1905.

> Excellent overview of the period of the question. It shows awareness of dates and overall understanding.

> This sentence balances the opening sentence and clearly states the candidate's own viewpoint.

The Emancipation of the Serfs in 1861 began the process of economic modernisation by freeing labour from centuries-old constraints and permitting change in the towns and the countryside. The results were not immediate since former serfs were held back by the redemption dues they were required to pay and the control of the mir which collected these, but ultimately emancipation allowed greater mobility of labour, which is an essential feature of economic modernisation.

> This paragraph is packed with relevant detail showing breadth of knowledge. However, the candidate has not been side-tracked into description. Instead, the examples of government intervention are used to support the opening comment that 'state capitalism' transformed the economy.

From the time of Alexander II, 'state capitalism' helped to transform the economy. This was practised by successive finance ministers — Reutern, Vyshnegradsky and Witte — who built up government finance to kick-start economic growth. Reutern successfully improved the collection and accounting of taxes (abolishing tax-farmers), extended credit facilities, gave government subsidies to businesses and encouraged foreign investment by offering government-guaranteed annual dividends. By 1881, Russia had thus already taken the first steps towards economic modernisation, creating a new economic infrastructure.

Vyshnegradsky and Witte took economic modernisation a stage further and were successful in promoting not only the further spread of the railways but also the growth of heavy industry, which had previously been neglected. Among their achievements were a much more widespread state-owned railway system and the 'show piece' Trans-Siberian railway. Huge industrial complexes were developed, including the Baku oilfields, which produced more than half the world's oil by 1901, while St Petersburg and Moscow were transformed into large industrial cities.

> Again, the knowledge and detail is impressive here.

However, the Tsarist governments were not entirely successful in their quest for economic modernisation. Their achievements were largely won at the expense of the peasants, who were driven too hard to provide grain for sale abroad, particularly by Vyshnegradsky. The peasant famine of 1891–1892 demonstrated the limitations of his policy and he was forced to resign. Nevertheless, Witte maintained a similar policy, oppressing the peasants with grain requisitions and high indirect taxation. This was not only socially ruinous; it also prevented improvement in agriculture and the growth of an internal market to stimulate industry.

This linking sentence opens the way for the balancing argument: the ways in which the Tsarist governments were not successful.

Economic modernisation was also reliant on foreigners — for capital and for their managerial and technical expertise. It was the wealth of the Nobel and Rothschild families, for example, that lay behind the expansion at Baku. Furthermore, the policy of unremitting industrialisation had caused huge social problems by 1905, with a discontented urban population, living and working in often appalling and unregulated conditions. There was no state-run workers' insurance and it was illegal for workers to strike.

This paragraph and the one before it show very clearly and directly the deficiencies of Tsarist policies. The final sentence shows an awareness of future change but the answer firmly remains within the dates specified in the question.

Moreover, the rural economy had failed to modernise to the same degree as industry. Although agriculture enjoyed a boom in the years immediately after emancipation, most farming remained small-scale. Population growth exacerbated the peasants' position and whilst a small class of kulaks benefited from buying out their poorer neighbours with the help of loans from the government Peasant Land Bank set up in 1885, for every peasant family that thrived, many more fell beneath the poverty line and became landless labourers.

Therefore, it would be fair to say that the Russian governments were only superficially successful in modernising the Russian economy in the years 1861 to 1905. They were hampered by their own disregard for the workforce — both urban and rural — and a narrow appreciation of what economic modernisation demanded. Whilst the statistics might look impressive, Russia only grew so substantially because it started from a very low point. Some important steps had been taken, but there was a considerable distance to go, particularly in the development of agriculture which still provided a livelihood for 80 to 90 per cent of the population.

This is a strong conclusion which repeats the view of the introduction and summarises the evidence on which that view has been based. It also pays due attention to the word 'modernise', showing that the question has been fully understood and addressed.

24/24

This is a very good answer. It responds explicitly to the words and dates of the question, offers plentiful comment backed by precise and detailed supporting information, balances success against failure in an analytical way and offers clear judgement. The view set out in the introduction is sustained through a series of well-structured and tightly focused paragraphs to provide a convincing response. It is therefore well deserving of full marks.

Reverse engineering

The best essays are based on careful plans. Read this essay and the examiner's comments and try to work out the general points of the plan used to write this essay. Once you have done this, note down the specific examples used to support each general point.

Section 3:
Russia in revolution, 1904–1906

The war with Japan and the causes of the 1905 Revolution

Background to the war

Both Russia and Japan wanted to expand into the decaying Chinese Empire. Russia sought coastline and ports; Japan sought land and resources for its growing population.

In 1898, the Chinese granted Russia a 25-year lease of the Liaodong peninsula, so that they could extend their **Trans-Siberian railway** southwards to Port Arthur, an ice-free port. The Japanese had briefly held Port Arthur in 1895 and regarded it as part of their sphere of influence. War broke out when, in January 1904, the Japanese attacked Port Arthur in an attempt to drive the Russians out.

Reasons why Russia went to war with Japan

- Industrialists and traders saw commercial opportunities in the Far East.
- Control of the Pacific coast offered security and was strategically advantageous.
- Cavalry officers and admirals were keen to show off their abilities and win glory.
- Nicholas disliked the Japanese and believed Russia would save the area from the 'yellow peril'; a prejudice which many Russians shared.
- Russia was suffering an economic depression with associated strikes and uprisings. War was a chance to engender patriotism.
- Plehve (Minister of Internal Affairs, 1902–1904) believed a 'short swift victorious war to stem the tide of revolution' would 'distract the attention of the masses from political questions'.

Outline of the war

2 January 1904– 22 December 1905	Japanese troops attacked and maintained a long siege of Port Arthur.
18 April 1904	Russian armies were heavily defeated along the Yalu River (the border between Manchuria and Korea).
February– March 1905	Russia suffered a major defeat at Mukden – 90,000 men were killed or wounded and the Russians were forced to abandon the town.
14/15 May 1905	24 of the 27 ships of the Russian Baltic fleet were sunk in the Straits of Tsushima, off the coast of Japan, in just 90 minutes by a superior Japanese fleet commanded by Admiral Togo, after having spent seven months sailing to Japan.

Results of the war

War was concluded at a peace conference arranged by US President Roosevelt in Portsmouth, USA on 23 August. Russia recognised Japan's sphere of influence and surrendered its lease on Port Arthur and its Liadong railways to the Japanese.

Reasons for the Russian defeat

- The war was 6000 miles from **St Petersburg** and it took six days for men and supplies to reach the front along the single track Trans-Siberian railway.
- The **Tsar** refused to send his best troops lest their absence encourage revolts in St Petersburg.
- Troops fought bravely but were badly led by over-confident and incompetent officers.
- Ammunition was in short supply.
- The Japanese had more modern weaponry and superior organisation.

Results of the Russian defeat

Defeat by an Asian power increased internal unrest and provoked feelings of shame and anger.

- Humiliation, since it was the first time in modern history an eastern country had defeated a European power. Press reports increased political opposition to Tsardom.
- Plehve was assassinated by social revolutionaries in July 1904.
- There were renewed **Zemstva** demands for a national assembly.
- Economic problems including food and fuel shortages in the cities. Prices rose and factories closed, creating mass unemployment.
- Wartime discontent led to a revolution in St Petersburg in 1905.

Prioritisation

Below are a sample exam-style 12 mark question and a list of reasons that could be used in the answer. Demonstrating prioritisation is one way of structuring the answer to an 'Explain why' question. Using your own knowledge and the information on the opposite page, decide the order of priority you would give to these factors. Write numbers on the spectrum below to indicate their relative importance and, beneath each, briefly justify that factor's placement, demonstrating why you feel some factors are more important than others.

Explain why the Russo-Japanese war provoked unrest in St Petersburg.

1. The Japanese were regarded as an inferior race.
2. The Japanese attack on Port Arthur appeared to be unprovoked aggression.
3. Large numbers of peasants were conscripted to fight in the army.
4. The Russian soldiers were defeated at Mukden with 90,000 deaths.
5. The Russo-Japanese war exacerbated existing economic problems.
6. Newspapers reported poor distribution of supplies and inadequate ammunition at the front.
7. The Russian Baltic fleet was sunk at Tsushima in 90 minutes.
8. Reports made it clear that the army was badly led and organised.

Most important   Least important

Develop the detail

Below are a sample exam-style 24 mark question and a paragraph written in answer to this. The paragraph contains a limited amount of detail. Annotate the paragraph to add additional detail to the answer.

How far was the outbreak of revolution in St Petersburg in 1905 due to Russia's failures in the Russo-Japanese war?

Russia's wartime failures certainly contributed to the discontent that led to the outbreak of revolution in St Petersburg in 1905. Firstly, the war proved an embarrassing humiliation for the Russian state. Secondly, it showed the chaotic nature of that state and how difficult it was to rule such a vast empire. The Tsarist government could not run the war effectively. Furthermore, the war created severe economic disruption which added to the discontent at home. The workers suffered badly and this is what provoked the 1905 revolution. Far from being the short victorious war that Plehve had promised, the Russo-Japanese War was a fairly lengthy and disastrous affair, which also brought about Plehve's own assassination in 1904.

The 1905 revolution: Bloody Sunday and developments up to October 1905

Revised

Bloody Sunday

On 3 January 1905, the dismissal of three workers who had joined **Father Gapon**'s union (see page 26) at the Putilov works in St Petersburg, escalated into a widespread strike.

On 9 January, Gapon organised a peaceful march (of around 20,000 workers) to the **Winter Palace**. They carried a petition for the Tsar asking for improvements in working conditions, more food and a **constituent assembly** with working-class representation. They blamed ministers for their problems and carried portraits of the Royal Family and icons. However, they were fired upon by armed police and mounted **Cossacks**. Officially, 130 were killed and 450 wounded, but journalists suggested 4600 deaths. The event became known as Bloody Sunday.

Results of Bloody Sunday

- Nicholas II, who had been absent, underestimated the event and told the workers' representatives whom he met 'for tea' that they had been misguided and should return to work. He replaced the moderate Mirskii with the hard-liner Bulygin as Minister of the Interior.
- Illegal unions formed, strikes spread and political meetings escalated.
- Grand Duke Sergei Alexandrovich, Nicholas's uncle and governor general of Moscow, was assassinated by social revolutionaries on 4 February 1905.
- On 18 February, Nicholas II created a committee to consider constitutional reform.
- An 'All-Russian Union of Railway Workers' was established in March and **soviets** of elected factory workers were formed to co-ordinate strikes.
- There was a naval mutiny on the battleship *Potemkin* – part of the Black Sea Fleet (14–24 June). The sailors took the boat to Odessa and gained the support of townsfolk. More than 2000 were killed there when the authorities tried to disperse sympathetic crowds.
- **Peasants** rioted and in August a 'Peasants' Union' was formed.
- On 6 August, Nicholas promised a restricted State Duma which revolutionaries regarded as too weak.
- A printers' strike in Moscow on 23 September spread to St Petersburg and other cities creating a general strike in October.

- Nicholas was forced to concede the October manifesto (17 October), promising reform.

Reactions to the events of 1905

There were four main opposition groups in 1905, each with their own aims and methods:

Liberals	National Minority Groups
• Demanded **civil rights** and a national assembly elected by **universal suffrage** with full legislative powers • Favoured a **constitutional monarchy** and at a meeting of Zemstva representatives in Moscow (April) urged Nicholas to take action to curb 'revolution' • Strongly supported in the universities • Formed professional unions (e.g. teachers, engineers) which combined in the 'Union of Unions' under '**Kadet**' leader Paul Milyukov (April).	• Jews demanded equal civil rights • Poles, Finns, Latvians and other ethnic groups demanded **political independence**, breaking up the Empire • Ukrainians voiced economic and political grievances in a general strike in Odessa in June • A Muslim Union Congress was held in August, demanding regional autonomy • In October the Peasant Union of Volokolamsk created an independent republic (which lasted until July 1906) • Racist '**Black Hundreds**' confronted ethnic protestors, inflicting beatings and hangings.
Socialist Revolutionaries (SRs)	**Social Democrats (SDs)**
• Wanted to destroy Tsardom • Carried out political assassinations • Supported an 'All-Russian Union of Peasants' to co-ordinate rural action • Were prominent in the St Petersburg Soviet but disagreed with the Social Democrats.	• Wanted a workers' revolution to overthrow Tsardom • Encouraged the formation of workers' soviets • Encouraged supporters to withhold taxes and withdraw bank deposits to cripple the government • Supported strikes and organised general strikes in October and November • **Mensheviks** dominated the St Petersburg Soviet, which Leon Trotsky chaired from October to December.

Long-term or short-term?

Below is a sample exam-style 12 mark question, which asks for a range of reasons. Understanding the difference between long-term and short-term factors helps give structure to an answer to an 'explain why' or 'why' question. The chart that follows offers a list of reasons that are relevant to the answer to the question. Using the information on the opposite page and your own knowledge, decide whether each reason should be considered a long- or short-term factor and tick the appropriate box.

Why did Father Gapon lead a march to the Winter Palace in 1905?

	LONG-TERM	SHORT-TERM
Because industrial workers had very poor living and working conditions		
To present a petition listing workers' grievances to the Tsar		
Because there was very little welfare legislation to protect workers in the city		
Because there was a strike at the Putilov works		
To ask for working-class representation in government		
Because Father Gapon had created an 'official' trade union		
Because the workers were loyal to the Tsar and felt Tsar Nicholas could and would help them		

 Delete as applicable

Below are a sample exam-style 24 mark question and a paragraph written in answer to this question. Read the paragraph and decide which option (underlined) is the most appropriate. Delete the less appropriate options and complete the paragraph by justifying your selection.

How successful was political opposition in bringing about the revolution in Russia in 1905?

In the months between January and October 1905, political opposition was <u>very successful/ fairly successful/only partially successful/not at all successful</u> in bringing about a revolution in Russia in 1905. Following the slaughter of Bloody Sunday in St Petersburg in January 1905, the more moderate liberals and national minority groups as well as the radical Socialist Revolutionaries and Social Democrats all sought to maintain the political agitation and press for constitutional change. There were strikes, uprisings, political meetings, petitions and mutinies in the following months, all fuelled by news of further disasters in the Russo-Japanese war. Before October 1905, the Liberals had <u>successfully/fairly successfully/unsuccessfully</u> managed/tried to ....

_____

The national minorities had <u>successfully/fairly successfully/unsuccessfully</u> managed/tried to ...

_____

At the same time the Socialist Revolutionaries had <u>successfully/fairly successfully/ unsuccessfully</u> managed/tried to ...

_____

While the Social Democrats had <u>successfully/fairly successfully/ unsuccessfully</u> managed/tried to ...

_____

The <u>successes/failures</u> of the opposition were because ...

_____

The October Manifesto and promise of reform

Reasons for the October Manifesto

On 17 October 1905, Nicholas issued a decree, promising constitutional reform. Its details were drawn up by Sergei Witte, chairman of the Council of Ministers. A number of factors lay behind it:

Long-term

- The failure of the **autocracy** to adapt politically as Russia had modernised economically.
- The poor living and working conditions breeding discontent among urban workers.
- The grievances of the peasantry who suffered low living standards, high taxation including the burden of redemption payments, a lack of land and continuing discrimination.
- The grievances of **national minorities** who had never been fully assimilated and had been subject to **Russification**.
- The resentment of middle-class professionals, who had been given power in the Zemstva but excluded from participation in a national government, which they perceived as incompetent.
- The despair of students and **intellectuals** at Russia's inability to modernise and promise a better future for its people.

Short-term

- The humiliation, economic disruption and feelings of helplessness engendered by the Russo-Japanese war.
- The economic slump and bad harvests which had led to greater hardship and food shortages in 1903–1904.
- Father Gapon's march and the events of Bloody Sunday, 9 January 1905.
- Tsarist **reaction** to Bloody Sunday: Nicholas's initial disinterest, reliance on repression and the reluctant offer of a purely consultative National **Duma** with a narrow franchise in August.
- The widespread agitation of 1905 – strikes, demonstrations, soviets, petitions and mutinies.
- The pressure of the political groups with their specific demands and in particular the growth in assertiveness of the Zemstva.

Immediate

- The rejection of the Tsarist proposals for a restricted Duma by a Conference of Zemstva representatives in September.

- The government's inability to control and repress the various opposition movements that were exerting pressure at the same time, e.g. the Petrograd Soviet co-ordinated the activities of Soviets in other cities whilst there was widespread rural disorder and concurrent demands for regional autonomy.
- The October General Strike brought the Russian economy to a standstill; uniting sympathetic employers and strikers and affecting officials in government ministries, e.g. employees in the Treasury and State Bank went on strike.
- The Tsar had too few loyal troops to repress disorder and run essential services. Mutinies affected a third of the army in European Russia and soldiers on the Trans-Siberian railway returning from the Russo-Japanese war in the Far East.
- The appointment of the moderate Sergei Witte who proposed the October Manifesto as the only way to preserve Tsardom, despite his own doubts about the wisdom of conceding Tsarist power.

Terms of the October Manifesto

The Manifesto created a 'constitutional monarchy' by permitting the establishment of a National Duma (parliament) to work with the Tsar in the governing of Russia. Its promises fulfilled most of the **Liberals'** demands, but there were also some important limitations to what it promised.

Promises	Limitations
• Civil liberties, such as freedom of conscience, speech, press and assembly for all • Universal suffrage • No law without the consent of the Duma.	• 'Freedom of speech' was open to differing interpretations • **Indirect elections** were to be established with separate elections for peasants, landowners and towns • Laws still required Nicholas's assent and it was not clear whether the Duma could initiate **legislation**.

Specific or underlying?

Below is a sample exam-style 12 mark question, which asks for a range of reasons. Understanding the difference between specific and more general or 'underlying' reasons helps give structure to an answer to an 'explain why' question. The chart that follows offers a list of reasons that are relevant to the answer to this question. Using the information on the previous page and your own knowledge, decide whether each reason should be considered a specific or underlying factor and tick the appropriate box.

Explain why Tsar Nicholas II was forced to grant concessions in October 1905.

	UNDERLYING	SPECIFIC
Growth of opposition movements		
A general strike which brought the economy to a standstill		
Hostility to Tsarist autocracy		
Discontent of workers and peasants		
Zemstva demands for a full State Duma		
Humiliation following defeat in the war against Japan		
The unreliability of the army		

You're the examiner

Below are a sample exam-style 24 mark question and a paragraph written in answer to this question. Read the paragraph, and the mark scheme provided on page 3. Decide which level you would award the paragraph. Write the level below, along with a justification for your decision.

How important was pressure from the Zemstva in persuading Nicholas II to grant the October Manifesto?

Nicholas II was more ready to respond to pressure from the Zemstva than that from the more radical Social Democrats and Socialist Revolutionaries, because he recognised the need to co-operate with these bodies of middle-class professionals, whose voices were influential in both the localities and the universities. Although Nicholas was not initially inclined to make any concessions, and demonstrated his commitment to autocracy in the dismissal of the more moderate Mirskii as Minister of Internal Affairs, he was prepared to allow Mirskii's successor, Bulyagin, to draw up proposals for an elected National Duma, thus showing some acceptance of the Zemstva's desires. However, Nicholas had hoped that this would be a purely consultative body, and it can only have been pressure from the Zemstva, which rejected it in September, that forced his change of mind in October. The Zemstva had grown far more organised in the course of 1905, holding regular national conferences from March and presenting Nicholas with continual petitions demanding civil and political rights, universal suffrage and an assembly with legislative powers. Such determination was also seen in the formation of the 'Union of Unions' under Milyukov in May 1905. However, Nicholas would never have conceded his October Manifesto had it not been for one basic fact. Nicholas knew the Zemstva could be won over by constitutional reform in a way that the radicals could not. The SRs and SDs were pledged to the overthrow of Tsardom and to counter that threat, Nicholas was prepared to bow to Zemstva pressure.

Level: Reason for choosing this level:

Repression and the recovery of Tsarist authority

The impact of the October Manifesto

Mass celebrations followed the issue of the manifesto, but its terms divided the opposition to the Tsar.

■ Moderate right-wing liberals known as Octobrists fully supported the proposals and formed the supportive 'Union of 17 October' under Guchkov.

■ More left-wing liberals known as 'Kadets' offered temporary acceptance and formed the Constitutional Democratic Party under Milyukov. They wanted a constituent assembly to draw up a new constitution but accepted the manifesto promises as a first step only.

■ The **Socialist Revolutionaries** and **Social Democrats** rejected the proposals and encouraged their supporters to participate in another general strike organised by the St Petersburg Soviet in November.

Not all sections of society were won over:

■ Many workers were sceptical of the promises and remained loyal to the radicals.

■ Soldiers and sailors continued protests about pay, conditions and treatment with further mutinies at **Kronstadt** (26–27 October) and Vladivostok (30–31 October).

■ Peasants' risings escalated with hopes of land redistribution. In November, a Peasants Union conference in Moscow demanded land reform. A decree announcing the end of redemption payments from January 1907 had no immediate effect.

■ National minority groups, particularly Poles, Finns and Jews, continued protests, fearing the promises would ignore them.

The recovery of Tsarist authority

Although pockets of resistance remained to be dealt with in the early months of 1906, by the end of 1905, the government was again in control.

Tsarist action/repression

■ In November 1905, the Union of Russian People was created (with funding from government officials) to fight against the radicals. Harsh penalties were brought in for 'criminal acts'. Arrests, exiles and summary executions helped break the general strikes.

■ Most army units and the Cossacks remained loyal and helped storm the St Petersburg and Moscow Soviets in November/December 1905. An uprising in Moscow (10–15 December) was crushed by an artillery barrage.

■ Troops and Black Hundreds restored order in the countryside with attacks on peasants, ethnic groups and **pogroms** of Jews.

Weaknesses of opposition

■ The loss of liberal support after the October Manifesto weakened opposition. Peter Struve, who joined the Kadets, said 'Thank God for the Tsar who has saved us from the people'.

■ The radicals had no clear leader; Leon Trotsky, chairman of the St Petersburg Soviet, was exiled to Siberia (November) and Lenin, who only returned from exile in November, fled to Finland in December.

■ The workers became less keen to maintain strikes as pay dwindled and the second General Strike (November) was called off after four days.

■ Peasants, whose main concern was land, were persuaded that the end of redemption payments would herald better times.

Make the links

Below are a sample exam-style 12 mark question and a series of relevant reasons that could be used in the answer. Read the question and add a comment and linking phrase to each reason to explain each reason and show how it relates to the following one.

Explain why unrest continued after the granting of the October Manifesto.

Reason	Comment and linking phrase leading to the next reason
Workers believed the manifesto granted them the right to speak out, form unions and strike; the peasants believed it gave them the right to take land; the soldiers and sailors believed it gave them an opportunity to air grievances openly.	
The Socialist Revolutionaries and the Social Democrats wanted complete revolution, with social change too. Lenin and Trotsky tried to maintain the fight.	
The army, police and the Black Hundreds were used to repress continued rebellion.	

Turning assertion into argument

Below are a sample exam-style 24 mark question and a series of assertions. Read the question and then add a justification to each of the assertions to turn it into a supported view, so creating an argument.

How far was the recovery of Tsarist authority in the years 1905–1906 due to repression?

The recovery of Tsarist authority was the result of the support given by the Octobrists and Kadets ...

_____

_____

The recovery of Tsarist authority was the result of the November decree of 1905 which abolished the peasants' redemption payments ...

_____

_____

The recovery of Tsarist authority was because opposition groups were divided, poorly organised and inadequately led ...

_____

_____

Exam focus

Below is a sample A grade essay for a 24 mark question. Read the essay and the examiner's comments around it.

How successful was Tsar Nicholas II in maintaining his authority in the years 1904 to 1905?

A well-directed opening which conveys a view and shows a very good understanding of the debate provoked by the question.

It would be untrue to say that Tsar Nicholas II was entirely successful in maintaining his authority in the years 1904 to 1905, because full Tsarist autocracy was destroyed when he granted the October Manifesto of 1905. Thereafter, the Tsar became, in theory at least, a constitutional monarch. However, despite the breakdown in government between Bloody Sunday in January and December 1905, the Tsar emerged with much of his power still intact at the end of the year and his authority, if not his autocracy, was little changed.

Notice how this sentence provides a relevant comment and a good deal of accurate and specific supporting detail.

Although defeat in the Russo-Japanese War spread anger and resentment in the capital, Nicholas II managed to maintain his authority despite the Putilov strike and the events of Bloody Sunday. It is likely that he totally underestimated the strength of the challenge he faced, but he acted calmly, summoning workers' representatives to his palace, feeding them, then telling them to go home. Nicholas neither made, nor had any intention of making, concessions. He replaced the moderate Mirskii with the hard-liner Bulygin and acted with complete authority ordering his police and army to take action to quell the rioting.

Notice the repeated use of the key word 'authority' which helps maintain focus and relevance.

The Tsar was less successful at maintaining his authority over the subsequent months as revolutionary action spread throughout the Russian Empire. The formation of illegal trade unions and the development of the soviets presented a direct challenge. The formation of the All-Russian Union of Railway workers, with the potential to bring the country to a standstill, in April, left Nicholas in a very difficult position. He briefly hoped that the victory of his Baltic fleet which arrived in the Tushima straits in May might relieve the pressure, but its defeat presented a further challenge. The mutiny aboard the Battleship Potemkin was the first significant display of disloyalty to the Tsar from the armed forces and could not easily be ignored. Without military support Tsar Nicholas II could easily have been left powerless.

This shows an appreciation of change over time, but skilfully avoids narrative.

This is a perceptive comment, adding depth to the answer.

However, although the Tsar was forced to make concessions in October 1905, in some respects, the granting of the October Manifesto was a means to the preservation of Tsarist authority. The Tsar agreed to the formation of a State Duma, but its powers were ill-defined. Likewise, he promised civil rights, but reserved for himself the interpretation of promises such as freedom of speech and freedom of assembly. In theory he appeared to give much away, but in practice, he retained considerable authority to use and interpret the manifesto as he saw fit.

Another thoughtful observation which offers an alternative interpretation.

Thanks to his timely concession in October, Tsar Nicholas II was mostly successful in reasserting Tsarist authority in the months between October and December 1905. He used the police, the Cossacks and the Black Hundreds to crush opposition groups, student demonstrators, ethnic rebels and Jews. He even resorted to an artillery barrage to end the power of the Moscow Soviet. The loyalty of the armed forces was therefore crucial for the recovery of Tsarist authority.

The successful reassertion of Nicholas' authority was also helped by divisions in the opposition. The moderate liberal Octobrists were supportive of the Tsar and even the less moderate liberal Kadets, who wanted further constitutional reform, were keen to see the disruptive popular risings brought to an end. Neither was prepared to intervene to stop the crushing of the St Petersburg and Moscow Soviets, making it more difficult for the Socialist Revolutionaries and Social Democrats to maintain the spirit of revolution after October 1905. The workers were practical men, with little care for the ideologies of Marxism. They grew tired of holding out on strike for little pay and none of the opponents of Tsardom had sufficient resources, leadership or military control to press home their demands.

The Tsar was also eventually successful in winning back authority in the countryside with his promise of November to end redemption payments. Although this did not take immediate effect and it took time for peasants to respond, it helped to weaken the power of the Congress of Peasant Unions and persuade the naturally conservative peasants that their interests were not those of the town workers and revolutionaries.

Although Tsar Nicholas II faced a considerable challenge to his authority in the years 1904–1905, he was relatively successful at maintaining his position. Although there was a brief moment in the middle months of 1905 when his authority seemed in question and, in October 1905, he issued his manifesto and accepted a National Duma, he nevertheless retained the power to interpret the promises of that manifesto and demonstrated his authority in the later months of that year. Clearly, Tsar Nicholas II was more of a success than a failure in maintaining his authority in the years 1904 to 1905.

This sentence leads into a balanced assessment of how authority was preserved.

The previous three paragraphs and that which follows show a good understanding of factors supporting the reassertion of authority and are well focused, clearly structured and supported.

The essay ends strongly with a focused conclusion that sums up the main argument of the essay.

24/24

This is an impressive answer which shows an understanding of debate and an excellent grasp of the subject matter. The candidate has advanced a personal judgement and upheld it through the answer, so that the conclusion flows naturally out of what has gone before. It would receive full marks.

Exam focus

This essay is successful because it maintains a strong focus on the question throughout. Go through the essay and underline every mention of the key word 'authority'. Note also how that key word is integrated into the commentary. Next look at an essay you have written and underline your use of key words. Can you improve on your own efforts in the light of what you have seen here?

Section 4:
The Tsarist regime, 1906–1914

The work of the Dumas

The new constitution

The October Manifesto promised reform, but no exact detail of how the new Russian constitution would work. The new structure, established in February 1906, comprised:

	Role:	Method of selection:
The Council of Ministers	It initiated and approved all **legislation**.	• It was appointed by the **Tsar**. • It was led by a prime minister. • It was responsible only to the Tsar.
The State Council	It debated laws and had to approve them.	• It was half elected by **Zemstva**, half appointed by the Tsar.
The State Duma	It debated laws and had to approve them.	• It had over 500 delegates, elected every five years by men over 25 using **indirect suffrage**.

Political groupings

Political parties were legalised in March 1906 for the elections but the **Bolsheviks**, the **Socialist Revolutionaries** and the extreme Nationalists refused to participate. The main groupings were:

Party	Policy	Mostly supported by ...
Octobrists	**liberal** reform	upper class/ big businessmen
Kadets (Constitutional Democrats) and Progressives	constitutional and liberal reform	middle class/ lesser businessmen
Conservatives and Nationalists	preservation of Tsarist power	upper classes
Social Democrats (SDs) – (Bolsheviks and **Mensheviks**)	workers' revolution	workers
Socialist Revolutionaries (SRs)	**socialism**/land redistribution	**peasants**
Trudoviks	**agrarian socialism**	peasants/**intelligentsia**
National minority and religious groups	independence	non-Russian/non-Orthodox peoples

Four days before the first State **Duma** met, the 'Fundamental Laws' were issued. They cleverly upheld the October promises, but confirmed the Tsar's power.

The 'Fundamental Laws' (23 April 1906)

These confirmed that the Tsar held:

- 'supreme **autocratic** power'
- power to initiate legislation and approve laws
- the right to appoint and dismiss ministers
- command of the armed forces
- responsibility for foreign relations
- the right to summon and dissolve the Duma
- power to rule by decree when the Duma was not in session (Article 87).

These laws would clearly undermine the powers of the promised Duma, by giving the Tsar the means to ignore its wishes.

Spider diagram

Below are a sample exam-style 12 mark question and the beginnings of a spider diagram to identify relevant reasons. Read the question and complete the spider diagram with a sentence of explanation. Then prioritise your reasons by adding numbers to each oval – with 1 as the most important reason and 7 as the least important.

Explain why Nicholas II issued the Fundamental Laws.

You're the examiner

Below are a sample exam-style 24 mark question and a paragraph written in answer to this question. Read the paragraph and the mark scheme provided on page 3. Decide which level you would award the paragraph. Write the level below, along with a justification for your decision.

How far did the new Russian constitution of 1906 weaken the Tsarist autocracy?

In 1906 a new Russian constitution was set up following the 1905 revolution which had forced Nicholas II to issue the October Manifesto promising change. It was meant to give the Russian people a more democratic government after all the troubles they had been through. It did not and instead allowed the Tsar to keep virtually all his power. The Fundamental Laws which were issued on the Tsar's instructions stated that he had 'supreme autocratic power', so it is quite wrong to say that the autocracy was weakened in any way. Under the new Russian constitution, the Tsar appointed the Council of Ministers and half the State Council. This means he still had autocratic power. Although a new State Duma was set up and this was elected, it was useless. Only the Council of Ministers was allowed to draw up laws and the Duma just debated them, which was not much of a concession. The Tsar could also dismiss the Duma and could then rule by decree when the Duma was not in session. This was complete autocracy. The Tsar also had power over the armed forces and foreign affairs, so his position was not changed at all.

Level: Reason for choosing this level:

_____

_____

Prime ministers and the Dumas

Revised

Prime ministers

Sergei Witte resigned as prime minister in May 1906, shortly after a 2250 million gold franc loan from France had been agreed in April to prop up the Tsarist regime. He was replaced by Ivan Goremykin, an opponent of political reform who found it impossible to work with the first Duma. Goremykin resigned in July 1906 and Pyotr Stolypin took over. Stolypin was assassinated by the SRs in 1911 and was replaced by Vladimir Kokovstov until 1914. All struggled to control the popular opinions voiced by the Dumas and reported in the national press.

The Dumas

There were four Dumas between 1906 and 1914.

First Duma (May–June 1906) – 'Duma of National Hopes'

- It was dominated by Kadets and radicals with a large peasant representation.
- It demanded radical constitutional change.
- It passed a vote of 'no confidence' in the government.
- It was dissolved but reassembled in Finland where Kadets issued the 1906 'Vyborg Appeal' for a tax boycott. Leaders were arrested and disenfranchised.

Second Duma (February–June 1907) – 'Duma of National Anger'

- Stolypin engineered elections to increase the number of Octobrists.
- However the Bolsheviks and the SRs participated, increasing the number of radical deputies.
- It opposed most Tsarist proposals including agrarian reform.
- Measures were passed under Article 87 when the Duma was not in session.
- Leading radicals were exiled after dissolution.

Third Duma (November 1907–June 1912) – 'Duma of Lords and Lackeys'

- By the 1907 Electoral Law, the representation of peasant, worker and **national minorities** was reduced. Consequently, Octobrists and Conservatives dominated.
- It agreed some social and agrarian reform but there were still some disputes with the Tsar.
- It was twice suspended and Article 87 was used.

Fourth Duma (November 1912–1917 (suspended 1915))

- The number of Octobrists decreased, creating a gulf between the conservatives and **socialists**.
- The right- and left-wing deputies could not co-operate and the fourth Duma was increasingly ignored.
- It voted for **war credits** in 1914, but was suspended in 1915 after demanding more power.

How important?

Below is a sample exam-style 24 mark question which asks you about the importance of a factor. Questions like this can be answered by balancing the way the factor was important against the ways in which it was not. A series of statements relevant to the question are given below. Using your own knowledge and the information on the previous pages, decide whether these statements suggest the factor was important or not important and tick the appropriate box.

How important was the contribution of the Dumas to the process of government in the years 1906–1914?

	IMPORTANT	NOT IMPORTANT
Dumas could be by-passed, suspended and Article 87 used, or dissolved by the Tsar.		
Nicholas appointed his own ministers, who formulated laws.		
The third Duma debated, amended and approved important agrarian reforms and other government proposals.		
The Tsar had to approve all laws.		
The Dumas acted as a channel of communication, allowing ministers to gauge popular opinion.		
The franchise could be changed to control Duma membership.		
There was a growth of political debate as the Duma proceedings were reported in the press.		

Identify an argument

Below are a sample exam-style 24 mark question and two sample paragraphs. One suggests a high-level answer because it advances a supported argument. The other suggests a low-level answer because it contains only description and assertion. Identify which is which. The definitions below should help you:

- **Argument**: giving a view supported by reasoning and fact
- **Assertion**: giving a view that is not supported by reasoning and fact
- **Description**: providing facts but not in support of a view.

How successful were the State Dumas in the years 1906–1914 in increasing democracy in Russia?

Paragraph 1

There were four state Dumas between 1906 and 1914. The first, known as the 'Duma of National Hopes' was dissolved when it expressed radical views. Some members tried to reassemble in Finland and they even appealed to the Russian people not to pay their taxes as a protest. However, their leaders were arrested . The Tsar did not want democracy. The second Duma was called the 'Duma of National Anger'. It was dismissed when it opposed Stolypin's proposals for agrarian reforms. The Tsar then used the powers of the Fundamental Laws to rule by decree while the Duma was not in session. The radicals were exiled and Stolypin changed the electoral law so that the next Duma would be easier to work with. However the Duma still had to be suspended twice. When there was no Duma, there was no democracy, but the fourth Duma lasted until 1914 so there was a little democracy in the end.

Paragraph 2

The State Dumas were only partially successful in increasing democracy in Russia. Giving the vote to all men over 25, holding elections every five years and allowing press reports on Duma debates all helped increase democracy. However, the Tsar still exercised an autocratic power and members of the first and second Dumas were arrested, exiled and disenfranchised when they tried to oppose the Tsar's wishes. Demands for radical change were met with suspensions and dissolutions. The Tsar's power to rule by decree when the Duma was not sitting was well used and the attempt of the first Duma members to meet in Finland was immediately stopped. The electoral law was also manipulated, firstly to increase the number of Octobrists in the second Duma and again to decrease peasant, worker and national minority representation before the third Duma. Such action was totally against the spirit of democracy and although the fourth Duma worked more effectively, it was less, not more democratic than that of 1906.

The agrarian reforms of Pyotr Stolypin

Background

Pyotr Stolypin, a former provincial governor, rose to prominence through his work in curbing rural discontent. He favoured hard-line methods and, as prime minister from 1906, established repressive **courts martial** to halt the disorder in the countryside. The hangman's noose became known as 'Stolypin's necktie' as over 60,000 were executed, imprisoned or exiled under Stolypin.

Nevertheless, he also believed that a radical reform of agriculture was required to prevent further peasant unrest. Stolypin referred to his programme as a 'wager on the strong and sober'. He wanted to increase individual peasant ownership so as to create a class of profit-orientated and politically conservative farmers who would support the regime. To facilitate this, some peasants would have to move to the towns and this would boost industry too.

Stolypin's legislation

The change proposed by Stolypin went against centuries of farming practice in Russia. Even after **emancipation**, peasants still farmed communally and worked scattered allotments which varied according to family size. The **mir** system and collective ownership of land by families was abolished by a decree of November 1906 and further reforms followed from 1906 to 1914 whereby:

- As promised in 1905, redemption payments were abolished in January 1907, and peasants became free to leave their villages.
- Peasants could apply for permission to consolidate scattered strips into single farms.
- More state and Crown land was made available for peasant purchase.
- A new peasant land bank was established to fund purchases.
- Government subsidies for migration to/settlement in Siberia were made available.

Stolypin suggested his proposals needed 20 years to work but they were cut short by war in 1914.

Successes of the legislation

- Peasant ownership of land increased from 20 per cent in 1905 to nearly 50 per cent in 1915.
- Grain production rose annually from 56 million tons in 1900 to 90 million tons by 1914.

- By 1909, Russia was the world's leading cereal exporter.
- Some peasants (known as **kulaks**) consolidated their land, often 'buying out' poorer peasants to create compact and more efficient and profitable peasant farms.
- Around 3.5 million peasants moved from over-populated areas to Siberia, creating a major agricultural region there for dairy and cereals.
- Some peasants sold out and moved to the towns to find work, so boosting the industrial labour supply.

Failures of the legislation

- Although the Land Organisation Commission was established, the bureaucracy involved made procedures slow; by 1913 only 1.3 million out of 5 million applications had been dealt with; by 1914 only around 10 per cent of land had been transferred from communal to private ownership.
- In 1914, 90 per cent of peasant holdings were still based on scattered strips. Peasants were still reluctant to change farming methods (increased productivity was a result of good harvests, for example in 1913 there was a record harvest).
- Some landowners tried to hold on to their lands and it proved difficult to divide up common land without protracted legal battles.
- The poorer peasants lost all their land and descended into deeper hardship.
- Amongst the landless labourers were those who were too old or too rooted to their communities to seek alternative work.
- Siberia proved difficult terrain for those who relocated there.
- Stolypin's reforms didn't address the key issue – the redistribution of land held by the **nobility** – and land hunger remained.

Turning statements into reasons

Below are a sample exam-style 12 mark question and a series of statements. Read the question and turn each of the statements into a relevant reason that could be used in the answer.

Explain why Stolypin promoted agrarian reform.

STATEMENT	REASON
The years 1903–1904 were known as the years of the Red Cockerel.	
Most Russian peasants had a very low standard of living.	
To encourage more peasants to move to towns to boost industrialisation.	
Most peasants lived and worked communally in the mirs.	
Siberia was underdeveloped and sparsely populated.	
1905 had seen violent agricultural as well as urban disturbances.	

Complete the paragraph

Below are a sample exam-style 24 mark question and the outline of a paragraph written in answer to this question. The paragraph begins with a relevant comment in relation to the question and ends with a further link. However, it lacks supporting examples. Complete the paragraph by providing some factual detail in the space provided.

How far did Stolypin's reforms transform Russian agriculture in the years 1906 to 1914?

Although Stolypin's reforms changed patterns of landholding, helping to create a prosperous kulak class and leading to the development of large-scale dairy and cereal production in Siberia, overall they never succeeded in revolutionising Russian agriculture in the way Stolypin had hoped. For example,

_____

_____

_____

_____

_____

_____

Stolypin's proposals were never given time to take effect because Stolypin himself was assassinated in 1911 and the war intervened to stop the changes in patterns of landholding which were underway. However, from the evidence available it would certainly be untrue to say that Russian agriculture had been transformed in the years 1906 to 1914.

Economic development in Russia up to 1914

Industrial growth

Despite an international trade recession which hit Russian heavy industry badly from around 1900, the domestic unrest of 1902–1906 and the strains of the 1904–1905 Russo-Japanese War, economic growth continued. State revenues doubled from 2 to 4 billion roubles in the years 1908 to 1914 and the number of industrial workers increased from 2.5 to 2.9 million. Russia experienced an annual growth rate of 8.5 per cent, making it the world's fifth largest industrial power by 1914.

Economic expansion still depended heavily on foreign loans, but proportionately internal investment increased. Government finance went into heavy industry after the Russo-Japanese war, boosting manufacturing, mining, transport and construction. By 1914, Russia had the second largest railway in the world, with 62,000 km of track, and long-haul domestic as well as foreign trade increased substantially. Russia was the world's fourth largest producer of coal, pig iron and steel, it was the second largest producer of oil and was fourth in gold-mining.

Light and newer industries also expanded with a growth in factories manufacturing chemicals, rubber and electrical equipment. The service industries such as banking, insurance and the civil service grew and the industrial infrastructure was strengthened. The number of banks more than doubled in the years 1908 to 1914. A relatively efficient stock market was created and big corporations, with monopolies over manufacture, became well established. For example, the coalfields of the south formed the 'Association of Southern Coal and Steel Producers', a **cartel** that controlled the market by establishing output quotas and fixing prices.

Social improvements

Industrial expansion was accompanied by some social improvements:

- **Trade unions** were legal from 1905, giving workers an opportunity to demand wage rises and other improvements.

- Some welfare legislation was passed. In 1912, a sickness and accident insurance scheme was established; factory inspectors were appointed.

- Spending on elementary education increased and by 1914, 50,000 primary schools had been established (an 85 per cent increase since 1905). Around 55 per cent of children were in full-time education and overall literacy rates increased to 40 per cent by 1914 (compared with 30 per cent in 1900).

- The Zemstva expanded welfare services in the localities.

Problems of industrial growth

- The Russian economy grew at a slower pace than other developing nations in the years 1908 to 1914. The main export was still grain and only 30 per cent of production was industrial, compared with 75 per cent for Britain and 70 per cent for Germany.

- Industrialisation created new business interests that formed political pressure groups and a resentful working class.

- Real wages (what workers could buy with earnings) declined in the years 1910 to 1913 because of inflation and an employers' squeeze on wages in the face of growing world competition; working and living conditions remained poor; opportunities for self-improvement were limited.

Revival of militancy

In 1912, workers at the Lena Goldfields (northern Siberia), demanding improvements to their accommodation, food, and long hours of work in inhospitable conditions, went on strike and around 500 were killed when the army intervened. This was one of over 2000 separate strikes across Russia in 1912. In 1913 there were 24,000 strikes and in 1914 over 1 million. Strike activity was encouraged by the Bolsheviks who infiltrated trade unions and were selling 40,000 copies of their *Pravda* newspaper by 1914. In July 1914, a general strike broke out in **St Petersburg**, but ended just before war began on 1 August.

Specific or underlying?

Below is a sample exam-style 12 mark question, which asks for a range of reasons. Understanding the difference between specific and more general or 'underlying' reasons helps give structure to an answer to an 'explain why' question. The chart that follows offers a list of reasons that are relevant to the answer to this question. Using the information on the previous page and your own knowledge, decide whether each reason should be considered a specific or underlying factor and tick the appropriate box.

Explain why miners went on strike at the Lena Goldfields in 1912.

	UNDERLYING	SPECIFIC
A militant workers' movement developed from 1912.		
The Lena miners had complaints about their accommodation, food and treatment.		
The Bolsheviks spread revolutionary propaganda and tried to co-ordinate strike activity.		
Wages had not risen as much as inflation in the years 1910 to 1913.		
The miners' long hours and conditions of work in an inhospitable climate were grim.		

 Identify an argument

Below are a sample exam-style 24 mark question and two sample paragraphs. One suggests a high-level answer because it advances a supported argument. The other suggests a low-level answer because it contains only description and assertion. Identify which is which. The definitions below should help you:

- **Argument**: giving a view supported by reasoning and fact
- **Assertion**: giving a view that is not supported by reasoning and fact
- **Description**: providing facts but not in support of a view.

How far did economic development in the years 1906–1914 help to strengthen the Russian State?

Paragraph 1

Although Russia's economic growth in the years 1906 to 1914 was impressive, it cannot be said that this unreservedly strengthened the Russian state. Economic development increased Russia's social problems as more workers were needed in industry and yet were given little legal or welfare protection. They were vulnerable to the whims of their employers, who were themselves keen to put profit above all else, as world competition increased. Workers' real wages declined because of inflation in the years 1910 to 1914 and their working and living conditions remained poor. Consequently, there was an undercurrent of industrial unrest which grew worse from 1912. Rather than strengthening the state, economic growth created a militant working-class body, receptive to revolutionary propaganda, particularly from the Bolsheviks, and with limited loyalty to a regime that seemed largely to ignore it. The Lena Goldfields massacre of 1912 reinforced the workers' feelings of isolation and vulnerability and did nothing to bolster the state.

Paragraph 2

Russia had a growth rate of 8.5 per cent between 1908 and 1913 and increasing investment boosted the expansion of the coal, iron, steel and oil industries in particular. Russia became the world's second largest producer of oil and fourth largest producer of coal, iron and steel. Russia was also fourth in gold-mining, although there was a strike at the Lena Goldfields in Siberia in 1912 and 500 workers were killed when the army opened fire. This was not the only industrial strike. The Bolsheviks helped to stir up strike activity and between 1912 and 1914 a spate of strikes spread across industrialised Russia. Most industrial workers lived and worked in poor conditions and had few opportunities for self-improvement. Levels of education were low, even though there had been some improvements under Stolypin. There was also a health insurance scheme for workers introduced in 1912 but resentments remained high.

The condition of Russia in 1914

It is difficult to reach a judgement about the condition of the Tsarist regime in 1914, because the outbreak of war that year brought a wave of patriotism that masked the tensions lying beneath the surface.

Politics

Positive	Negative
• A National Duma had been established, appeasing the liberals / middle classes.	• The Tsar had issued the Fundamental Laws and the 1907 Electoral Law. • There was little co-operation from Dumas, e.g. the 1906 Vyborg Appeal.
• The third Duma worked with Stolypin to pass agrarian and social reforms.	• Disputes persisted despite electoral management.
• There was no significant opposition by 1914, thanks to repression and the use of the **Okhrana**. • Radical leaders, e.g. Lenin, were exiled.	• Radical opposition from the SDs and the SRs survived, e.g. SR assassinations, including Stolypin 1911; wide circulation of *Pravda* among workers. • Opposition was only held at bay by repression – 'Stolypin's necktie'.
• The regime was politically stable.	• The Tsar was detached and conservative. • **Reactionary** ministers ignored even moderate demands and continued discrimination against ethnic groups. • The support base for the regime was very narrow.

Economic

Positive	Negative
• Economic growth averaged 8.5 per cent per annum from 1908 to 1914. • Russia was the world's fifth largest industrial power.	• Russia was growing more slowly than other developed nations. • Industrial development brought social disquiet.
• Growth was more firmly based on internal rather than foreign investment.	• There was still considerable reliance on overseas investment and expertise, e.g. from France.
• Stolypin introduced major agrarian reforms. • There was a record harvest in 1913.	• Only around 10 per cent of Russian land was consolidated. • Good harvests disguised the backward farming methods.

Social

Positive	Negative
• There was an 85 per cent increase in primary school provision from 1905 to 1914 and a 40 per cent literacy rate.	• Only 55 per cent of children were in full-time education and there was a 60 per cent illiteracy rate.
• There were welfare reforms, e.g. Sickness and Accident Insurance reform of 1912.	• There were appalling living/working conditions in industrial towns.
• There was expansion of the professions – doctors, lawyers, teachers.	• There were too few doctors and teachers in rural areas.
• The trade unions were legalised.	• Strikes escalated 1912–1914, e.g. Lena Goldfield's Strike in 1912. • General Strike in St Petersburg in 1914 gave the Bolsheviks a platform from which to spread views. • Unions did not help the majority in rural areas.
• Agrarian reforms created a wealthy kulak class.	• Advances were slow and for every peasant that grew richer, another became poorer.
• There was massive public support for the Romanov Tercentenary of 1913 and outbreak of war, 1914.	• Patriotic fervour was more for Russia than the Tsarist **autocracy**. • There was widespread disapproval of the influence of **Rasputin** over Nicholas and **Alexandra**. (Rasputin was a peasant faith-healer/monk who appeared able to stem Nicholas' son Alexis' **haemophilia**. Rasputin's drunkenness and womanising raised passions against the 'mad monk'.)

Below are a sample exam-style 24 mark question and a paragraph written in answer to it. Read the paragraph and identify parts that are not directly relevant or helpful to the question. Draw a line through the information that is irrelevant and justify your deletions in the margin.

How far had the hopes of the Zemstva deputies of 1905 been fulfilled by 1914?

Although the Zemstva deputies had hoped that Nicholas would develop into a modern constitutional monarch, these hopes had not been fulfilled. Instead, the Tsar had grown increasingly detached, intent on preserving his God-given powers as expressed in the Fundamental Laws of 1906 and ignoring the complaints of the National Dumas. Nicholas was a weak-willed man, who had never wanted to be tsar. Nicholas and Alexandra celebrated the tercentenary of the reign in 1913. Nicholas and Alexandra held a spate of balls and dinners as well as travelling in great pomp across their empire, making a triumphal entry into Moscow on a white horse. The praise he received reinforced his belief that he was loved by his people and that those demanding constitutional change were misguided. Nicholas also allowed Rasputin considerable influence at court and over Church and state appointments. Rasputin was a faith-healer who appeared able to control Nicholas' son Alexis's haemophilia, but he was also a drunkard and a womaniser. Haemophilia is a disease that prevents the blood from clotting and Alexandra had become infatuated with this 'mad monk'. Rasputin's corrupt influence undermined the Zemstva's hopes for a more democratic government still further.

Below are a sample exam-style 24 mark question and a paragraph written in answer to this. The paragraph contains a limited amount of detail. Annotate the paragraph to add additional detail to the answer.

How successful was the Tsarist government in restoring stability in the years 1905–1914?

In many ways the Tsarist government failed to restore stability despite the absence of any further revolution after the momentous events of 1905. There were four different National Dumas and this constant swapping and changing meant that the national government was far from stable. Each Duma had its own ideas and complaints and dealing with opposition took up a good deal of time. There were many different political parties too, and they all had their own ideas about the different issues the Dumas considered. There were also Tsarist ministers, who had their own separate views. Government was therefore unstable and it was hard to get much done. In addition there was lots of unrest among the broad masses of the population. The peasants were not satisfied with the reforms that were attempted, while the industrial workers became even more militant. Government almost broke down in the last few years before the war which was a sign that the Tsarist government had not been very successful in restoring stability.

Exam focus

Below is a sample A grade answer for a 12 mark question. Read the answer, the brief plan and the examiner's comments around it.

Explain why the first two Dumas of 1906–1907 broke down.

Choosing a thematic approach will help to avoid a chronological and over-descriptive answer.

> **Plan**
>
> Thematic approach:
>
> - Underlying lack of co-operation
>
> - Problems Tsar/Dumas
>
> - Problems within Dumas
>
> The breakdown of the Dumas of 1906 to 1907 was fundamentally because they were a new experiment in government which depended on a degree of co-operation which neither the Tsar and his ministers, nor the deputies were used to. The Tsar had always ruled in an autocratic fashion, repressing views which conflicted with his own. Similarly, the new Duma deputies came largely from a background of 'opposition' (many from the Zemstva or parties formed during the conflict of 1905) and were equally unable to adopt a conciliatory line. When the Tsar replaced the more reformist Witte by the conservative Goremykin in 1906, he sent a message to the Duma that his government was intending to stand firm and the subsequent appointment of the hard-liner Stolypin reinforced this. The deputies resented this and fought back, for example issuing the Vyborg Appeal for a tax boycott after the dissolution of the first Duma.
>
> Unsurprisingly, the division of opinion both between the Duma and the Tsarist ministers led to conflicts over policy-making. The majority of moderate deputies in the first two Dumas had expected to have the opportunity to discuss further constitutional reform, while the Tsar simply regarded the Dumas as a vehicle for rubber-stamping decrees such as Stolypin's agrarian reform proposals. Thanks to the constitutional arrangements, when the Duma deputies tried to submit the Tsarist proposals to scrutiny, the Tsarist regime was able to fall back on the emergency powers permitted by Article 87 and so could pass legislation as it always had done. Put simply, the first two Dumas broke down because the Tsar possessed the power to dissolve and by-pass them.
>
> The lack of co-operation also extended to the many different political groupings within the Dumas. There were major differences in the views of the deputies which made any decisions difficult. The first Duma was overwhelmingly radical-liberal because neither the Bolsheviks nor the Socialist Revolutionaries to the left, nor the extreme Nationalists on the right, chose to participate. Nevertheless, there was still a wide spectrum of opinion from radicals to conservatives. The second Duma was even more

This paragraph is well focused and deals clearly with the issue of co-operation. Notice the use of 'fundamentally' in the first line, which advances the underlying theme.

This paragraph effectively combines the practical reasons for the ending of the first two Dumas with the linking theme of lack of co-operation between the Dumas and the Tsarist ministers.

This paragraph advances another aspect of lack of co-operation by looking at the internal composition of the Dumas.

divided, with the left-wing radicals winning seats, sabotaging debate and refusing to listen to those on the right. Furthermore, government action to disenfranchise the moderate Kadets, following their appeal after the first Duma reduced the influence of the centre-ground liberals. It is little wonder that the second Duma also broke down.

The first two Dumas of 1906–1907 broke down because of a lack of co-operation between the Dumas and the regime and within the Dumas themselves. Neither the Tsar nor the deputies were satisfied with the institution. The Tsar never wanted it and many deputies believed its place in the broader framework of government was too limited or, in the case of the radicals, irrelevant. In such circumstances both Dumas collapsed since it simply proved impossible to get sufficient co-operation to get anything done.

There is direct reference to the wording of the question here, keeping this answer well focused.

The answer ends with a direct summary conclusion. It does not waste words but emphasises the underlying and interlinking factors of lack of co-operation to show good overall understanding.

12/12

This is a very good answer which provides an underlying factor and develops this with reference to more specific reasons. By emphasising the importance of lack of co-operation throughout, it shows a high level of understanding of the interlinking factors and it ends with a strong summary conclusion.

Using examples

Whenever you write an answer to a 12 mark question, you should ensure that your ideas are supported by precise examples. This answer contains examples and detail to support the comments throughout. Using the headings given in the plan above, make a list of the factual examples that have been used to support each idea.

Section 5:
The First World War and the revolutions of 1917

The impact of the First World War

Revised

Military defeats

Germany declared war on Russia on 19 July 1914. As the vast Russian army was assembled, a surge of patriotism swept the country. Strikes ceased and the **Duma** voted for **war credits**. An All-Russian Zemstvo Union for the Relief of Sick and Wounded Soldiers was created at the end of July with **Prince Lvov** (a **Kadet**) as president and in August, **St Petersburg** was renamed as 'Petrograd' to sound less German. The country was divided into military zones, civilian authority was suspended and the sale of alcohol was forbidden.

Despite some initial successes on the Austrian front in August 1914, the invasion of East Prussia met strong German resistance and defeats were inflicted at:

- The Battle of Tannenburg (August 1914) which left 300,000 Russian soldiers dead or wounded
- The Battle of Masurian Lakes (September 1914).

A massive retreat began on both the German and Austrian fronts and reports of inadequate clothing and footwear and a shortage of food and munitions (e.g. two rifles to every three soldiers) were published.

The political impact of the war 1915–1916

- The **Zemstva** resented their loss of authority when they were doing more for medical relief than the government.
- Local and national industries assumed responsibility for supplies in the absence of **Tsarist** action. This encouraged political ambitions.
- The Zemstva and Duma accused the government of incompetence, for example pointing to the futility of the alcohol ban as **peasants** brewed their own.
- In August 1915, Kadets, Octobrists, Progressives and even conservative Nationalists in the Duma formed the 'Progressive bloc', demanding a change of ministers and constitutional reform. Disgruntled workers began more strikes in Petrograd.

- On 23 August 1915, the Tsar took over as commander-in-chief of the armed forces. He suspended the Duma and moved to the military headquarters at Mogilev. The war effort rallied slightly in 1916, as soldiers were better trained and supplies improved (rifle production doubled and heavy artillery production quadrupled). However, military success proved illusive.

- Nicholas was held responsible for the failure of the Brusilov offensive (June–August 1916). A lack of trained officers and Russia's underdeveloped railway network contributed to the defeat which sapped morale and provoked desertions.

- **Alexandra** (a German and intensely unpopular) and **Rasputin** assumed much influence over government and political appointments in Nicholas' absence. Rumours spread that they were sabotaging the Russian war effort and confidence in the regime fell. Rodzianko (President of the fourth Duma, which reconvened in February 1916) warned Nicholas but he did not respond. Rasputin was assassinated by Prince Yusupov in December 1916.

The economic and social impact of the war

The war drained Russia. Costs rose from 1500 million roubles in 1914 to 14,500 million by 1918, while production slumped as workers and peasants were **conscripted** to fight. Industrial capacity was lost as Poland and Western Russia were overrun by the Germans and naval blockades ended Russia's Baltic and Black Sea trade. There were vital distribution inefficiencies, partly due to the inadequate railway system which was disrupted by fuel shortages, but also because railways were prioritised for soldiers and military supplies, leaving food destined for civilians to rot in railway sidings.

Peasants made the situation worse by hoarding grain because there was nothing to buy, whilst workers suffered unemployment as non-military factories were forced to close due to lack of raw materials. Petrograd in particular, where there was a 300 per cent rise in the cost of living, saw an escalation of strikes.

Creating a Venn diagram

Below is a sample exam-style 12 mark question.
Use your own knowledge and the information on the
opposite page to produce a Venn diagram plan for
an answer to this question which groups the reasons
thematically.

Explain why the impact of war, in the years
1914 to 1915, posed problems for the Tsarist
government.

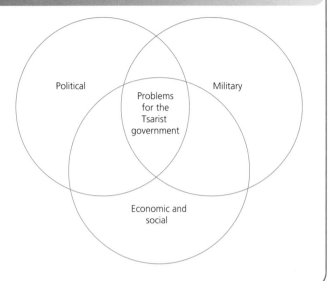

Delete as applicable

Below are a sample exam-style 24 mark question and a paragraph written in answer to this question. Read the
paragraph and decide which option (underlined) is the most appropriate. Delete the less appropriate options and
complete the paragraph by justifying your selection.

How far was military failure responsible for weakening the Tsarist regime in the years 1914 to 1916?

Military failure was <u>the most important reason/ an important reason/ just one of many
reasons</u> for the weakening of the Tsarist government in the years 1914 to 1916. Despite the
surge in Tsarist support that greeted the declaration of war in July 1914, a spate of battle
failures and military organisational incompetence soon weakened the government. Early
defeats and reports from the front line <u>made a huge difference to/ affected/ scarcely
affected</u> the public's perception of the government in 1914 to 1915. It was Nicholas's
decision to make himself commander-in-chief of the armed forces in September 1915
that <u>added to the already extensive discontent/made the crucial difference/was primarily
responsible for a weakening of government</u>.

_____

_____

_____

_____

The February/March 1917 Revolution

Matters came to a head in Petrograd in the winter of 1917 when starvation and desperation produced a workers' revolution.

Timeline of the events of January–February 1917

- 9 January: 150,000 workers demonstrated in Petrograd on the anniversary of Bloody Sunday (see page 32).
- 14 February: 100,000 workers from 58 factories were on strike; the Duma reassembled again and demanded the abdication of the Tsar.
- 19 February: news that bread would be rationed from 1 March brought panic buying and some violence in bakers' queues.
- 22 February: 20,000 workers from Putilov Works went on strike.
- 23 February: a march of women on International Women's Day was swelled by striking workers and militant students; around 200,000 demonstrators calling for bread and reforms appeared on the streets and police struggled to restore order.
- 24–25 February: demonstrations grew more menacing during these 'February days' as more joined in, and cries for bread were replaced by condemnation of the Tsar. Factories, shops and restaurants were closed. Cossack troops fought the police to protect the protestors.
- 26 February: Nicholas (who had failed to grasp the significance of the riots) authorised the use of troops. Some fired on protestors but mutinies began later in the day. Nicholas also ordered the closure of the Duma and it refused. Rodzianko asked for a new government, but Nicholas ignored his telegram.
- 27 February: the Petrograd garrison mutinied and joined protestors – arming them by seizing the arsenals; the crowd attacked police and released political prisoners. The Duma ignored the Tsar and formed a provisional committee to take control. The Petrograd **Soviet** of Workers' Deputies was created.
- 28 February: Nicholas II left his military headquarters to return to Petrograd; his train was diverted to Pskov. His ministers were arrested on the authority of the Provisional Committee. The Petrograd Soviet issued '**Order No. 1**' (a charter of soldiers' rights). This proclaimed Soviet authority over the army and encouraged the formation of soldiers' soviets. Sailors mutinied in **Kronstadt**.

The Tsar's abdication

- 1 March: The Duma and the Soviet agreed to support the creation of a **Provisional Government**.
- 2 March: The Soviet expanded to include representatives of the soldiers' soviets and the Provisional Government was established with Prince Lvov as prime minister. Army generals who had lost faith in the Tsar gave support to the new Provisional Government and halted troops marching on the capital to restore order. Encouraged by his ministers and generals, the Tsar abdicated in favour of his brother, Grand Duke Mikhail. (He believed his son Alexis was too weak to inherit the throne.)
- 3 March: Mikhail rejected the throne, leaving the Provisional Government and Petrograd Soviet in charge. The Tsar and his family were placed under house arrest, together with most of the Council of Ministers.

Over the next month, the revolution spread across Russia and local dumas (public committees) replaced the Tsarist government and police officials, while workers and soldiers created soviets to run their factories and battalions.

Make the links

Below are a sample exam-style 12 mark question and a series of relevant reasons that could be used in the answer. Read the question and add a comment and linking phrase to each reason to explain each reason and show how it relates to the following one.

Explain why rioting broke out in Petrograd in February 1917.

Reason	Comment and linking phrase leading to the next reason
Factory closures and disputes had put a lot of men on the streets at the time of the International Women's Day march on 23 February.	
The working classes in Petrograd were in a desperate economic situation. Adding to their down-trodden pre-war position, the war had brought a huge rise in the cost of living.	
The military effort, under the command of Tsar Nicholas II, was going badly and the Duma had demanded the Tsar's abdication.	

Specific or underlying?

Below is a sample exam-style 12 mark question, which asks for a range of reasons. Understanding the difference between specific and more general or 'underlying' reasons helps give structure to an answer to an 'explain why' question. The chart that follows offers a list of reasons that are relevant to the answer to this question. Using the information on the previous page and your own knowledge, decide whether each reason should be considered a specific or underlying factor and tick the appropriate box.

Explain why Nicholas II abdicated in March 1917.

	UNDERLYING	SPECIFIC
Nicholas was a stubborn but weak man with little idea of how to rule his vast empire.		
The Duma had grown exasperated with Nicholas' failure to appreciate the significance of the Petrograd riots.		
The Tsarist government had missed the opportunity to transform itself in 1905.		
The Russian war effort was disastrous.		
The army generals lost faith in Nicholas and the armed forces mutinied.		
Nicholas allowed Alexandra to influence him and gave Rasputin (up to 1916) and Alexandra too much influence over the Petrograd government during the war.		

Russia and the Provisional Government

The new authorities

After the Tsar's abdication, Russia was left with two 'ruling' authorities: the Provisional Government and the Soviet of Workers' and Soldiers' Deputies (The Petrograd Soviet). The Soviet (which provided some democratic legitimacy) agreed to accept the Provisional Government's authority until a **constituent assembly** could be elected to draw up a new constitution. This arrangement was known as the **Dual Authority** or **Dual Power**.

- Prince Lvov became prime minister with a government comprising mainly **liberal** Octobrists and Kadets.
- Alexander **Kerensky**, who sat on the executive committee of the Petrograd Soviet, was the only **socialist** in the new government.
- The Petrograd Soviet was mainly comprised of radicals, especially SRs and **Mensheviks** and acted as a 'guardian' of the rights of workers and soldiers.

Immediate changes

The Dual Authority issued decrees which allowed:

- civil liberties (for civilians and soldiers)
- the abolition of legal restrictions based on class, nationality or religion
- an amnesty for political, military and religious prisoners
- the abolition of capital punishment and exile
- the appointment of independent judges
- self-government for the army

- the right of the Petrograd garrison to retain weapons.

Other changes included:

- the imprisonment of Tsarist officials
- the appointment of 'liberal' **Commissars** to replace provincial governors
- the disbanding of the secret police and lifting of censorship
- the establishment of soviets in towns and the countryside
- independence for the Poles (behind German lines); other nationalities were told to await a constituent assembly.

Reactions to the Provisional Government

The hopes and democratic principles of the new Provisional Government were compromised by the demands of war. The fighting continued and in April, the Foreign Minister Milyukov secretly confirmed Russia's war aims to the allies so as to ensure the continuance of wartime loans. The leaking of this news led to mass public demonstrations, forced Milyukov's resignation and brought five socialists into the government in May. The early supporters of 'revolution' were rapidly disillusioned by what the Provisional Government offered, and by its insistence that the Russian people had to wait for a new elected constituent assembly before any major **legislation** could be enacted. The table below outlines the policy of the Provisional Government and reactions to it.

Group	Provisional Government's policy	Reaction
Peasants	• The setting up of land committees in April to collect information on land-holding. • New grain requisitioning scheme introduced the option of offering higher payments but retaining grain appropriations. • Wartime conscription continued.	• Initial enthusiasm turned to frustration in the absence of any official land redistribution. This led to an escalation in (sometimes violent) peasant seizures of land and property from the **nobility**, Church and wealthy **kulaks**. This activity was encouraged by radical agitators and peasants soon regarded the Provisional Government as a 'middle-class' government which favoured the landowners.
Workers	• Factory committees (soviets) and conciliation chambers were established to represent workers' interests. • There was support for employers' efforts to restore discipline. Employers could dismiss unco-operative workers and demand more than an 8-hour day.	• Soviets created a greater sense of working-class solidarity and protests continued. Food shortages, inflation and unemployment remained and in some cases got worse, so strikes continued (175,000 in June 1917). Factory owners felt the government was not doing enough.
Soldiers	• Soldiers' committees were established and aristocratic controls were reduced but limited immediate change was felt.	• Desertions increased (365,000 in March–May 1917 as opposed to 195,000 in August 1914–March 1917). • Soldiers believed Order No. 1 gave them the right to ignore the Provisional Government if the Soviet disagreed with it.

Prioritisation

Below are a sample exam-style 12 mark question and a list of reasons that could be used in the answer. Demonstrating prioritisation is one way of structuring the answer to an 'Explain why' question. Using your own knowledge and the information on the opposite page, decide the order of priority you would give to these factors. Write numbers on the spectrum below to indicate their relative importance and, beneath each, briefly justify that factor's placement, demonstrating why you feel some factors are more important than others.

Explain why most peasants failed to support the Provisional Government.

1. Agitators encouraged peasant resistance.

2. Peasants believed the Provisional Government was a middle-class government which favoured the landowners.

3. Most peasants were poor and uneducated and only concerned about their own livelihoods, not matters of national importance.

4. Peasants resented heavy grain requisitioning.

5. Peasants were not granted the land they believed should rightfully belong to them.

6. The Provisional Government was slow to set up land committees to investigate issues of land ownership.

7. The Provisional Government wanted the Russian people to wait for a new elected constituent assembly before major legislation was enacted.

8. Conscription for war continued.

Most important   Least important

 You're the examiner

Below are a sample exam-style 24 mark question and a paragraph written in answer to this question. Read the paragraph, and the mark scheme provided on page 3. Decide which level you would award the paragraph. Write the level below, along with a justification for your decision.

How important was the creation of the Dual Authority in weakening the government in Russia after February 1917?

The new Provisional Government had to share power with the Soviet of Workers' and Soldiers' Deputies which was also set up at the time of the Tsar's abdication. Under the Soviet's Order No. 1, the soldiers would only obey the Provisional Government if the Soviet agreed with its proposals, so the Provisional Government was restricted in what it could do. The Provisional Government needed the support of the soldiers to carry out its policies. The Soviet was elected so it could claim to have democratic power. It could control the factories and services, like electricity. It acted as a check on the Provisional Government's actions. Kerensky was the only person to sit in both the Soviet and Provisional Government in March 1917, so he was able to take messages backwards and forwards. The Soviet was led by socialists who wanted more concessions for the workers and land for the peasants. They did not want to wait until a constituent assembly met, like the Provisional Government did. However, it was mainly the moderate SRs and the Mensheviks that sat in the Soviet, so they were prepared to offer some co-operation.

Level: Reason for choosing this level:

Lenin and the Provisional Government April–July 1917

> ### Lenin
>
> Lenin was in exile in Switzerland when he heard of the Tsar's abdication. He had been in almost permanent exile since his release from Siberia in 1901, returning only briefly in October 1905. Nevertheless, he had continued to direct his **Bolshevik** followers, raising money, training agents, and writing books, articles and letters. After February 1917, Lenin was desperate to return to Russia to help shape its future. The Germans, hoping Lenin's presence would help end the war on the Eastern Front, provided a **sealed train** for Lenin and 27 other Bolsheviks to travel to Petrograd.

The April Theses

Lenin arrived at Petrograd's Finland Station on 3 April 1917 and was greeted by workers as a hero. He gave a rousing speech which was later published as the 'April Theses'. He demanded all power be given to the soviets and promised to work for 'peace, bread and land'.

Lenin's theses, while based on his own **Marxist** beliefs, were essentially an acceptance of the peasant takeover of land and a propagandist move, stating what Russians wanted to hear. They helped unite Bolsheviks under his leadership, although he initially struggled to win over the Central Committee of the Bolshevik Party to his belief in non-co-operation with the Provisional Government. Lenin worked tirelessly to expand the party, which had only 26,000 members in April. The Bolsheviks were still in the minority at the first 'All-Russian Congress of Soviets' (3–24 June) in Petrograd, but the failure of the Provisional Government's **June Offensive** helped Lenin's cause. It brought new demonstrations against the war and an increase in Bolshevik support from soldiers.

The July days

By July, Lenin had been joined by the determined Trotsky who had returned from exile in May. However, an armed **insurrection** by soldiers, Kronstadt sailors and factory workers in Petrograd on 3–4 July, which attracted some Bolshevik followers, threatened to undermine Lenin's efforts. The Provisional Government used troops to break up the protest. *Pravda* was closed down and some prominent Bolsheviks were arrested as a warning. Trotsky was among these, but Lenin managed to escape to Finland.

The Kornilov Affair

In July, Kerensky succeeded Lvov as prime minister and General Kornilov replaced Brusilov as commander-in-chief. Kornilov believed he could restore strong government and persuaded Kerensky to disband regiments involved in the July days and reduce the size of the Kronstadt base. He also suggested tougher penalties on workers who failed to supply military equipment, a ban on strikes and factory meetings, military control of the railways and sending troublesome workers to fight. To bring these into effect, he prepared to bring loyal troops to Petrograd (later claiming an agreement with Kerensky which the latter denied).

Kerensky opposed Kornilov's 'coup' of 25–30 August. He moved the Tsar and his family to Tobolsk and asked the Petrograd Soviet to help defend the city. Bolsheviks were given weapons and challenged the approaching army. Railway workers halted trains carrying troops to the capital and persuaded them to desert while Kerensky had Kornilov relieved of his post and arrested.

The Kornilov Affair increased popular radicalism. It increased support for the Bolsheviks and weakened Kerensky's position. The Bolshevik leaders were released from prison and strikes reached another high, with a three-day, 700,000 strong railway workers' protest in September.

Spider diagram

Below are a sample exam-style 12 mark question and the beginnings of a spider diagram to identify relevant reasons. Read the question and complete the spider diagram with a sentence of explanation. Then prioritise your reasons by adding numbers to each oval – with 1 as the most important reason and 6 as the least important.

Explain why Lenin issued the April Theses in 1917.

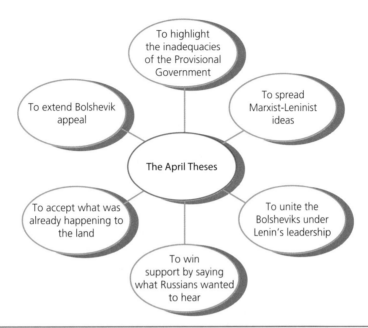

Turning assertion into argument

Below are a sample exam-style 24 mark question and a series of assertions. Read the question and then add a justification to each of the assertions to turn it into a supported view, so creating an argument.

How far were the problems faced by the Provisional Government by July 1917 due to the continuation of the war?

The deteriorating economic situation was largely the result of wartime dislocation because

_____

The continuation of war helped to radicalise the peasants, soldiers and workers because

_____

It was the failure of the Russian June offensive that led to the July days, which challenged the Provisional Government's authority because

_____

The October/November 1917 Revolution

The Bolsheviks, who had refused any compromise with the increasingly unpopular Provisional Government, grew at the expense of the Mensheviks and the SRs who urged national unity and therefore continued to work with the Provisional Government. In September, the Bolsheviks gained a majority on both the Moscow and Petrograd Soviets, where Trotsky became chairman (25 September). By October, the Bolshevik Party:

- had a membership of 200,000
- had a force of 10,000 Red Guards
- produced 41 newspapers.

Lenin wrote articles and produced policy decrees from Finland and from mid-September urged a seizure of power. However, the Bolshevik Central Committee (particularly Zinoviev and Kamenev) were reluctant to lead an uprising against the Provisional Government without a **mandate** from an elected constituent assembly. Trotsky suggested seeking all-socialist support at the Second Congress of Soviets, due on 25–26 October.

Moves to revolution, October 1917

- 7 October: Lenin returned secretly to Petrograd. Kerensky, fearing uprisings, ordered army units known to contain radical soldiers whom he considered untrustworthy to leave Petrograd.
- 9 October: The Petrograd Soviet set up a Military Revolutionary Committee (MRC) under Trotsky and Dzerzhinsky. It claimed responsibility for the defence of Petrograd. Soviet-appointed commissars were sent to army units.
- 10 October: Lenin won a Central Committee vote to replace the Provisional Government with the Petrograd Soviet, 10–2 (Zinoviev and Kamenev against).
- 10–23 October: The MRC gained control over the **Red Guards**, Petrograd and Peter and Paul Fortress Garrisons and Kronstadt sailors.
- 24 October: Kerensky tried to arrest MRC leaders and ordered the closure of Bolshevik printers. Around 8000 Bolshevik Red Guards and Kronstadt sailors seized key positions in Petrograd (telephone exchanges, post offices, railway stations, news agencies, state bank,

bridges and power stations). Kerensky fled and other government members met in an emergency session at the **Winter Palace**.

The October Revolution

- 25 October: The seizure of power in the name of the All-Russian Congress of Soviets was announced in the Petrograd Soviet. In the evening, Red Guards surrounded the Winter Palace; the battleship *Aurora* and St Peter and Paul fortress garrison fired some warning shots.
- 26 October: Red Guards and civilians broke into the Winter Palace (which was poorly defended by cadets and women) and arrested the remaining members of the Provisional Government.

The Congress of Soviets was asked to approve a Lenin-led government of political commissars, called '**Sovnarkom**' with power to rule by decree without reference to the Soviet. Lenin chose exclusively Bolshevik commissars to avoid power-sharing with other socialists. Mensheviks and right wing SRs walked out in protest, leaving Lenin with majority support.

These events might be seen as a Bolshevik '**coup d'état**', although propaganda described them as a popular uprising. Trotsky's role was also underplayed in comparison with Lenin's in later years.

Consolidating the Revolution

- 25 October–3 November: Soviet power spread across Russia, under Bolsheviks or other socialist groups. There were ten days of fighting in Moscow and some resistance elsewhere but much was peaceful.
- 26 October: the Decree on Peace called for an immediate end to the war; the Decree on Land declared all land to be the property of the people.
- 29 October: Kerensky tried to return to Petrograd but his forces were beaten by the Bolsheviks on the outskirts.
- November: ranks and titles were abolished; peace negotiations began.
- December: the Cheka (Bolshevik secret police) was set up.

How important?

Below is a sample exam-style 24 mark question which asks you about the importance of a factor. Questions like this can be answered by balancing the way the factor was important against the ways in which it was not. A series of statements relevant to the question are given below. Using your own knowledge and the information on the previous pages, decide whether these statements suggest the factor was important or not important and tick the appropriate box.

How important was Trotsky for the success of the Bolshevik Revolution of 1917?

	IMPORTANT	NOT IMPORTANT
Trotsky controlled the Red Guards.		
The Bolshevik Party had grown rapidly during the summer of 1917.		
Large numbers of Russians favoured a soviet takeover.		
The strategy employed on 24–25 October 1917 was very successful.		
Lenin continually urged the Bolshevik Central Committee to take action from mid-September.		
The Provisional Government was very weak and had few defenders.		
Trotsky suggested making an uprising coincide with the Second Congress of Soviets.		
Trotsky was Chairman of the Petrograd Soviet and one of the leaders of the MRC.		

Long-term or short-term?

Below is a sample exam-style 12 mark question, which asks for a range of reasons. Understanding the difference between long-term and short-term factors helps give structure to an answer to an 'explain why' question. The chart that follows offers a list of reasons that are relevant to the answer to the question. Using the information on the opposite page and your own knowledge, decide whether each reason should be considered a long- or a short-term factor and tick the appropriate box.

Explain why Sovnarkom was set up in October 1917.

	LONG-TERM	SHORT-TERM
The failures of the Provisional Government necessitated a new style of government.		
Lenin wanted to establish an exclusively Bolshevik government.		
It was essential to set up a new government without delay in order to address Russia's problems.		
The Petrograd Soviet in 1917 had been dominated by moderate Mensheviks and Socialist Revolutionaries.		
Lenin was determined to establish a body that could rule by decree without going to the Soviet.		
Lenin did not believe in power-sharing with other socialists.		
The Bolsheviks had split with the Mensheviks because they favoured a strong professional leadership and a less democratic party.		

Exam focus

Below is a sample A grade answer for a 24 mark question. Read the essay and the examiner's comments around it.

How far was the overthrow of the Provisional Government in October 1917 due to its own weaknesses?

This begins with a direct comment setting out a view in relation to the question. It also defines 'weaknesses' in a highly effective way. Notice how the view is also repeated in the final sentence of the paragraph. This provides for a wide-ranging and full answer.

This is a focused opening sentence with a comment on one aspect of weakness, which is subsequently explained. Further examples of structural weaknesses follow.

This sentence makes it clear that the structural weaknesses have been addressed and the candidate is going on to explain policy weaknesses. This is a good way of linking ideas.

The opening sentence introduces the strategic weaknesses and provides several specific examples to back it up.

The weaknesses of the Provisional Government were the main reason for the government's overthrow in October 1917. Weaknesses in structure, policies and strategy left it vulnerable to the attack of the Bolsheviks who, although small in number, were a highly motivated and well-organised force. Inspired by Lenin's leadership and disciplined by Trotsky's tactics, the Bolsheviks were able to topple the weak Provisional Government with virtually no bloodshed.

Structurally, the Provisional Government was weakened by the need to share power with the Petrograd Soviet. This prevented it from taking firm action to curb socialist opposition. It was also liable to the charge of being undemocratic, having emerged from the remnants of the fourth Duma, and being too 'middle class'. This made it difficult for its leaders, Prince Lvov up to July, then Kerensky, to win widespread appeal. Furthermore, neither showed much judgement. For example, Kerensky panicked over the Kornilov affair and gave arms to the Bolsheviks.

As well as structural weaknesses, the Provisional Government made some poor policy decisions. Regarding itself as temporary, it refused to make long-term policies, but also failed to call an early constituent assembly. Although it would have been difficult to conclude the war with Germany without reparations and loss of land, mounting a new offensive in June and permitting the Germans to take more Russian territory was another grave mistake. The government ignored land redistribution and seemed incapable of preventing military desertions and land seizures. It refused greater autonomy to national minorities and its limited reforms, for example the abolition of legal restrictions by class, nationality or religion, held limited appeal for workers who were more concerned with their immediate economic circumstances.

The Provisional Government also displayed strategic weaknesses in October 1917. Kerensky's attempt to forestall Bolshevik action by sending radical army units away from the capital unwittingly legitimised the establishment of the Soviet Military Revolutionary Committee which helped lead the revolution. Trying to forestall a popular uprising by, for example, closing Bolshevik printers, only fuelled revolution. Kerensky had no loyal troops to fall back on and foolishly fled the city when the Bolshevik challenge was imminent. Leaderless, the remainder of the government readily surrendered. When Kerensky tried to return, the Bolsheviks were established and he was repulsed.

However, it was not only its own weaknesses that brought about the Provisional Government's overthrow. Matched against these were the strengths of the Bolsheviks. Their policies, leadership and organisation all helped them to seize control in October. Lenin had, in his April Theses, sent out the message that they were ready to give land to the peasants, food to the workers, peace to all and power to the soviets. Their policies, spread by some effective propaganda, were in tune with what the Russians wanted.

Lenin proved a single-minded leader. He insisted on non-cooperation with the Provisional Government and inspired devoted followers not only among the workers, but also crucially in the ranks of the army and navy whose support was vital in October. It was Lenin too who forced his party's central membership to take action, although Trotsky's part in building up the Red Guard and providing the tactical organisation for the revolution should not be underestimated.

Bolshevik organisation ranging from the seizure of key communication centres before taking the Winter Palace, to the tactic of seizing power in the name of the All-Russian Congress of Soviets, was largely thanks to Trotsky's efforts. The development of the MRC and the discipline of the troops were vital for success, particularly since the Bolsheviks could still command limited support outside the two major cities of Petrograd and Moscow.

Although the problems of the Provisional Government were primarily the result of long-standing issues, exacerbated by the war, that does not excuse major weaknesses in the government's structure, policies and strategy. These offered a unique opportunity for the Bolsheviks. The strength of the Bolsheviks in terms of policies, leadership and organisation contributed to their success. However, it was Kerensky's failure to appreciate and counter those strengths that was ultimately to blame for the overthrow of the Provisional Government and it is therefore the weaknesses of that government that were responsible for the successful Bolshevik coup.

Here the candidate demonstrates an awareness of alternative factors and so opens the way for a balanced assessment. This paragraph addresses Bolshevik strengths in general, introducing what follows.

This and the following paragraph address the Bolsheviks' leadership and organisation in a logical fashion.

The conclusion sums up what has been said, repeating the view put forward in the introduction and also adding a comment on Kerensky which demonstrates depth of understanding.

24/24

This is an impressive answer that would receive full marks in Level 5. It is exceptionally well structured and maintains a coherent and well-supported argument throughout. It shows balanced evaluation, judgement and conceptual depth.

What makes a good answer?

You have now read three sample 24 mark grade A essays (see also pages 28–29 and 38–39). Use these essays to make a bullet point list of the characteristics of an A grade essay. Use this list when planning and writing your own essays.

Glossary

Agrarian socialism A belief that the land of the country belonged to the people and should be farmed co-operatively – working and selling the produce jointly, so supporting one another.

Alexander Herzen A radical member of the intelligentsia who believed in a socialist system based on the mir within a central governmental regime.

Alexandra German wife of Nicholas II.

Autocratic/Autocracy The possession of total power by one person; the ruler's word is law.

Black Hundreds Violent gangs which were part of the Union of the Russian People – a conservative, ultra-nationalist and anti-semitic group.

Black soil A belt of fertile agrarian land which stretches from the Ukraine to Siberia.

Bolshevik Party A Communist party that seized power in Russia in October 1917. After the Social Democratic Workers' Party split in 1903, Lenin led the 'Bolshevik' faction which believed in leadership by a small group of determined revolutionaries.

Bureaucrats Civil servants who undertake adminstrative tasks.

Cartel A grouping of industries protecting their own interests, for example fixing prices and the distribution of materials.

Civil rights Personal rights of, for example, freedom of speech, movement and religion.

Commissars Socialist government ministers.

Conscript Forced service, for example, in the army.

Constituent assembly A governing body that will draw up a new constitution.

Constitutional monarchy A monarchy in which the ruler's power is limited by an elected assembly.

Cossacks Men from South Russia who acted as cavalry for the Tsar.

Council of State (Tsarist) A body of advisers and ministers chosen by the Tsar. In 1906 this was replaced by a half-elected council of state.

Coup d'état An overthrow of government.

Courts martial Military courts which could order military punishments (usually harsher than those in civilian courts).

Crimean War A war in 1853–1856 provoked by Russian plans to expand into the Turkish-controlled Balkan area. The British and French fought on Turkey's behalf against Russia. Most fighting took place on the Russian Crimean peninsular which extends into the Black Sea.

Dual Authority A power-sharing arrangement in 1917 between the Provisional Government and the Petrograd Soviet. The former formed the government while the latter tried to ensure that the interests of the proletariat were advanced and protected.

Duma The Russian term for an elected council. Originally a duma was a municipal council but between 1905 and 1917 the Duma became the elected legislative council of state.

Emancipation Freedom; in the Russian context this often refers to the Ukase (edict) which gave the serfs their freedom.

Father Gapon An Orthodox priest who organised workers' unions from 1903 but remained loyal to the Tsar. He fled into exile after Bloody Sunday but returned in 1906 and was hanged either by SRs or the Okhrana.

Gendarmerie Uniformed security police from the nobility.

Haemophilia A medical condition whereby the blood does not clot. Consequently, internal bleeding can be fatal.

Import tariffs Monetary duties paid to the state when goods were brought into the country.

Indirect elections A voting system whereby individuals voted for representatives, who in turn voted for a smaller number to sit in an assembly.

Indirect suffrage The right to vote in indirect elections.

Indirect taxation Payment of a monetary duty to the state on goods or services.

Insurrection A riot or rebellion.

Intelligentsia/Intellectuals The educated upper class or middle-class elites who were often critical of the Tsarist regime.

Interest rates The percentage charge made on loans.

June offensive An attempt by the Provisional Government to drive the Germans back and win back land for Russia in 1917. It was a failure as the Russian supply lines became overstretched.

Kadets Supporters of the Constitutional Democrat Party who accepted the October Manifesto (1905) as a first step towards constitutional reform.

Kerensky A lawyer and a Socialist Revolutionary who sat in the Petrograd Soviet and Provisional Government in 1917, rising to become leader of that government from July. He was deposed by the Bolsheviks in October and eventually settled in the USA.

Kronstadt An important naval base just outside St Petersburg/Petrograd.

Kulaks Wealthy peasant farmers who owned land and employed labour.

Land Captains Noble officials with extensive local powers, including the right to over-rule the local Zemstva.

Land and Liberty An organisation derived from Populism, believing land should be divided between the peasants.

Legislation Laws.

Liberal Those wanting more personal and economic freedom. This term was often applied to those in favour of representative, elected government.

Mandate The legal right to do or control something.

Marxism/Marxist A political ideology derived from the theories of Karl Marx who taught that all history is driven by economic forces which creates class struggles. By the late nineteenth and early twentieth centuries, most Marxists wanted to progress to the stage of history whereby the proletariat (workers) would rise against the bourgeoisie (capitalists).

Menshevik Party After the Social Democratic Workers' Party split in 1903, Martov led the Mensheviks who favoured a broad membership and wanted to wait for a middle-class (bourgeois) revolution before a communist (proletarian) revolution took place.

Mikhail Bakunin An intellectual socialist and anarchist who wanted to remove the central government and create an independent agrarian socialist system.

Military colonies Settlements where army conscripts and their families were forced to live under a system of harsh military discipline.

Mir A Russian village commune where the peasants lived and worked.

Mortgage Borrowing money against some form of security, such as property. If the money is not repaid with interest, that security can be seized by the creditor.

Narodnik The Russian name for a populist. This literally means 'to the people' (see Populism in the right-hand column).

National minorities People of different ethnic or national backgrounds, such as Poles, Finns, Ukrainians and Jews, who lived within the state of Imperial Russia.

Nihilism/Nihilists Those who wanted to sweep away everything from the past.

Nikolai Chernyshevsky A socialist intellectual who edited the journal, 'The Contemporary' and wrote *What Is To Be Done?* in 1864, inciting peasants to rebel.

Nobility The highest members of society. This was an inherited position. Their income usually depended on wealth from land rents and they enjoyed privileges, including tax exemptions.

Obruk/Obrok Rent paid by serfs to their landlords for the land they farmed.

Okhrana The Tsarist secret police force which replaced the Third Section in 1880.

Order No 1 A charter of soldiers' rights providing for every unit to elect a committee to replace former officers and a deputy to the Petrograd Soviet which assumed political control over the army.

Peasants A class of people, mainly former serfs, who made up the bulk of the Russian population. They lived by farming in the countryside.

Pogrom An attack on Jews – often accompanied by arson, raping and looting.

Political independence Having the right to run one's own territory as a separate state with its own government.

Poll tax A tax payable by every adult serf/peasant.

Populism A belief in the power of the people (i.e. peasants) to bring about change by working together in the commune to create a new society.

Prince Lvov Prince Lvov was a wealthy aristocratic landowner who had led the Kadets and Russian Union of Zemstva before becoming leader of the Provisional Government in 1917. He retired in July because he could not control its mixture of liberals and socialists.

Provisional Government The government which emerged out of the Duma and held power in a dual power/dual authority arrangement with the Petrograd Soviet from February until October 1917. Its declared aim was to arrange for elections to a constituent assembly which would draw up a new constitution for Russia.

Pyotr Lavrov A populist who, in 1874, led a group of students into the countyside to live, and spread their ideas, among the peasants.

Rasputin A mystic peasant who believed redemption came through sin and seemed able to exert a hypnotic power which enabled him to curb the bleeding of Nicholas and Alexandra's haemophilliac son Alexis. He became very influential in government, particularly after Nicholas left for the war front in 1915, but was so unpopular he was assassinated in 1916.

Reaction/Reactionary Backward-looking behaviour which meant returning to former (conservative) ways.

Red Guards Bolshevik armed forces.

Russification The practice of enforcing Russian language and culture on national minority groups, while repressing their own ethnicity.

Russo-Turkish war Fought between 1877 and 1878 in support of the Balkan States challenging Turkish rule. Russia was successful and in March 1878, gained influence over an enlarged Bulgaria. However, Britain and Austria–Hungary forced the division of Bulgaria at the Treaty of Berlin (July) which undermined Russia's achievements.

Salt tax A monetary duty paid by non-nobles on the purchase of salt – an essential commodity.

Sealed train A train with the doors locked and windows covered to hide who was inside. No door could be opened until it reached its destination.

Serfdom The practice of having legally 'bound' peasants, who were the property of their landlords.

Serfs Agricultural labourers who were the personal property of their masters and could be bought and sold. There were various categories of serfs before 1861, including state serfs, household serfs and privately owned serfs.

Sergei Nechaev A radical peasant, dedicated and revolutionary, who inspired the Chaikovsky Circle which spread populist ideas and was behind Lavrov's attempt to 'go to the people'.

Show trials A propagandist trial in front of an audience for a political purpose.

Slavophiles Members of the Russian intelligentsia who believed Russia should seek a basis for its future development in its native traditions and not follow the western model.

Socialist Someone who believed in socialism – that factories and land should belong to the people.

Social Democratic Workers' Party A Marxist Party founded in Minsk in 1898. In 1903 it split into the two factions, the Bolsheviks and the Mensheviks.

Socialist Revolutionary Party A party built on populism and founded in 1901. It supported land redistribution between peasants but also believed that the urban proletariat could lead revolution. It advocated terrorist methods including assassination.

Soviet An elected council, usually of workers, soldiers, sailors and perhaps peasants, which controlled a factory or a local area. A soviet was set up in St Petersburg (by Trotsky) in 1905 and in 1917 the new Petrograd Soviet shared dual power/dual authority with the Provisional Government.

Sovnarkom The Soviet Council of People's Commissars, a committee which led Lenin's government after the October Revolution.

St Petersburg The capital of Russia (known as Petrograd from 1914).

State capitalism The attempt to direct economic modernisation 'from above'.

Strip-farming A feudal system of farming the land to share out better and poorer land, whereby each worker got a selection of strips in different fields to farm.

Third Section The state security network which used spies to keep a tight watch on the population.

Trade unions Organisations which represent workers in negotiations with employers. Before 1905 these were illegal in Russia.

Trans-Siberian railway This was built between 1891 and 1902 (with some subsequent additions) to connect Moscow in the west with Vladivostok in the east. It stretched across 7000 km and passed through Southern Siberia.

Tsar The title given to the Emperor of Russia. It derives from the Latin word 'Caesar' and means 'Emperor'.

Ukase A type of law, an edict or decree issued on the Tsar's authority.

Universal suffrage The vote for all adults (in the nineteenth century this usually meant the vote for all men).

Volosts Local administrative areas which supervised the mirs and (from 1863) had their own courts.

War credits Special taxes/loans granted in war time. Government bonds would provide creditors with interest payments while providing the state with money to fight.

Westernisers Members of the Russian intelligentsia who believed Russia should develop along the lines followed by western nations.

White-collar workers Those who worked in offices, shops and in professional jobs, such as teachers, bankers and retailers. They worked with their brains rather than their hands.

Winter Palace The home of the Tsar in the centre of St Petersburg (Petrograd).

Zemstva Elected local government assemblies set up in Russia in 1864.

Timeline

1855	Alexander II becomes Tsar.
1861	Abolition of Serfdom.
1863	Polish Revolt.
1864	Zemstva formed.
1874	Populists begin campaign to 'Go to the People'.
1877–8	Russo-Turkish war.
1881	Assassination of Alexander II.
1887–92	Ivan Vyshnegradsky is Minister of Finance.
1891–2	Widespread famine.
1892 –1903	Sergei Witte is Minister of Finance – rapid industrialisation programme.
1894	Death of Alexander III; accession of Nicholas II.
1898	Foundation of Russian Social Democratic Workers' Party.
1901–5	Economic slump follows worldwide depression and failed harvests; agrarian and industrial unrest.
1903	Split of Social Democrats at their Brussels Congress into Bolsheviks (led by Lenin), and Mensheviks (led by Martov).
1904	War breaks out between Russia and Japan over Korea and Northern Manchuria.
1905	January – 'Bloody Sunday' massacre leads to revolutionary upheavals.
	August – Portsmouth (USA) peace treaty with Japan.
	October – In his manifesto, the Tsar authorises elections to a State Duma; the St Petersburg Soviet is formed.
1906–11	Stolypin carries through programme of agrarian reform.

1912	Lena Goldfields Massacre – renewed industrial unrest.
1914	1 August – Germany declares war on Russia.
1915	6 September – Tsar assumes command of the armed forces and suspends the Duma.
1916	February – Fourth Duma reconvened. June – August – Brusilov offensive (failed). December – Rasputin assassinated.
1917	February – Strikes and civil unrest in Petrograd.
	23 February – International Women's Day march in Petrograd turns into a workers' demonstration.
	27 February – Troops refuse to fire on demonstrators and join the revolutionary movement; formation of the Petrograd Soviet.
	1 March – First Provisional Government is formed.
	2 March – Tsar abdicates.
	3 April – Lenin returns and formulates his April Theses.
	3–4 July – Anti-government demonstrations in Petrograd – the 'July Days'.
	27–30 July – Kornilov's coup fails and Red Guards are given arms.
	24–25 October – Bolsheviks seize key buildings in Petrograd.
	25–27 October – Provisional Government members are arrested; Bolshevik government announced; decrees on peace and land.
	December – Establishment of the Cheka.

Page 5, Long-term or short-term?

	LONG-TERM	SHORT-TERM
There was pressure from the educated classes and intellectuals to bring about change in Russia.	✓	
The state had a 54 million rouble debt.		✓
Autocratic government depended on the services of the nobility, who had grown lazy and dependent on serfs.	✓	
There was an escalation in peasant uprisings during the Crimean War.		✓
Nicholas and Dmitri Milyutin were enlightened bureaucrats who served Alexander II.		✓
Russia was economically underdeveloped.	✓	
Russia's military incompetence had been shown during the Crimean War.		✓

Page 5, Identify an argument

Paragraph 2 contains the argument; paragraph 1 is descriptive.

Page 7, Complete the paragraph: suggested answer

Although the 1861 Ukase allowed privately owned serfs to enjoy many legal freedoms, such as the right to marry whom they chose, run businesses, own property and travel, in many respects the Russian peasants were little better off. **Certainly the first two years were little different since the freed serfs had to perform two years of labour service before they became free. Even after this, however, the former serfs were required to make redemption payments for the land they were given and until these were paid, they had to remain in their mir. This effectively condemned them to a lifestyle that was little different from that they had previously known. Furthermore, the land was often overpriced by corrupt local landowning officials, leaving the former serfs in considerable debt, whilst allocations varied and could be inadequate. Without the use of the meadows, pasture and woodland, which went to the landowners, some peasants had barely enough to live on.** Consequently, methods of farming did not significantly improve and the number of peasants able to travel to nearby towns and work in industry was limited. This restricted the opportunities the Ukase might have been expected to give the peasants in order to improve their standard of living.

Page 7, Prioritisation: suggested answer

Most important   Least important

4 Peasants believed the land was theirs.	1 Peasants expected immediate freedom.	3 Peasants lost what they had previously had.	7 Peasants found themselves in considerable debt.	8 Peasants were, in part, left vulnerable.	2 This was less of a concern as they were used to living and working in the mir.	6 This was less of a concern as they were used to mir supervision.	5 This did not directly affect the peasants.

Page 9, Turning statements into reasons: suggested answer

STATEMENT	REASON
Serfdom was abolished in 1861.	A new way of creating an army was necessary.
Russia lost the Crimean War of 1853–1856.	The old system of creating an army had been shown to be inefficient and unsuccessful.
Most Russian peasants were illiterate.	An efficient army needed more educated soldiers.
Conscription for all over 20 became compulsory in 1874.	It was not possible or desirable to keep all those free men eligible for military service in one place.
Maintaining the Russian army was very expensive for the state.	Military colonies had proved very expensive to run.
In 1874, length of service was reduced from 25 to 15 years, 9 years of which were spent 'in reserve'.	Military colonies were not practical for only 9 years of active service.

Page 9, Delete as applicable: suggested answer

The Emancipation of the Serfs was **just one of many reasons** for the military, local government and judicial reforms of 1864–1874. Serf emancipation meant that a new system of military recruitment was needed to replace serf conscription and that the landlords' jurisdiction in the countryside had to be replaced by a new arrangement. The establishment of rural councils together with the setting up of local and volost courts **was connected with** the changes brought about by serf emancipation. This is because **it was no longer possible to ignore the rights of the freed peasants. However, the military reforms were as much the result of the catastrophes of the Crimean War and the liberal thinking of Dmitri Milyutin as the product of emancipation. Similarly, the reason for the local government and judicial reforms can be said to have come from the demands of the intelligentsia and the Tsar's own concerns that Russia should catch up with the West. Since the peasants had limited representation on the Zemstva and still had their own volost courts, it cannot be said that either of these measures was primarily designed to serve or respond to peasant needs.**

Page 11, Eliminate irrelevance

Among the reforms that transformed Russian society were changes in education. The changes were introduced by Alexander II's Education Minister, Golovnin who, ~~like the Milyutin brothers,~~ had liberal ideas. The educational changes came to an end when Golovnin was replaced by the conservative Tolstoy in 1866. In 1864, the new Zemstva were given responsibility for the provision of education in their own areas. These Zemstva were elected councils chosen by the nobles, townspeople, Church and peasants, ~~although voting was arranged in a way that allowed the nobles more influence.~~ The schools they established were made available to all, regardless of sex or background, which helped transform society, even though the poor rarely got beyond primary level. ~~Although the serfs had been emancipated in 1861, many were still very poor and reliant on subsistence farming.~~ The educational curriculum was also expanded with new scientific subjects and vocational secondary schools offering opportunities for advancement. ~~There was still a very small middle class in Russia though.~~ The universities were made self-governing which gave them more control over appointments and the courses they offered. This transformed society by creating a new group of critical and radical students.

Page 11, Develop the detail: suggested answer

Alexander II's economic reforms went some way towards making Russia a 'modern' state. **They reorganised government finances and made the Russian economy more efficient. More importantly still,** the government took responsibility for the development of industry, **providing some of the financing and contracts needed to get industry growing. The railways in particular benefited from this direction and there was some major growth in the country's infrastructure. Foreign** investment was also encouraged, **with the government giving a helping hand.** All this capital **enabled Russian resources to be exploited more fully,** although the expansion was still slower than its promoters hoped for. **The limitations of Russian society meant that** despite all the encouragement, Russia was still predominantly rural and undeveloped at the time of Alexander's death in 1881.

Page 13, Creating a Venn diagram: suggested answer

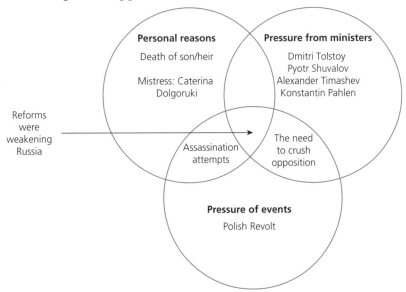

Page 13, You're the examiner

This paragraph would be awarded a borderline Level 4 mark. It shows explicit understanding and a good range of detail, with some balanced argument. However, it lacks the precision needed for a higher mark with, for example, exaggerated phrases like 'no more reforms', 'all the previous reforms came to an end' and 'let his ministers do as they wished'. Some parts are also less focused.

Page 15, Spider diagram: suggested content

Growth of opposition

1 **Censorship laws:** relaxation of censorship allowed works of Socialist intellectuals to spread.

2 **New ideas:** radical journals and books circulated and Marxism entered the country.

3 **Education changes** led to a larger and more independent student population.

4 **Local government changes** gave hopes of greater representation nationally and allowed middle-class intellectuals to debate views.

5 **Judicial changes** gave opportunities for more trained lawyers to express new ideas.

6 **Repression:** from 1866, disappointment increased demands for change.

Page 15, Turning assertion into argument: suggested answer

The growth of opposition was the result of Alexander II's judicial reforms **because they promoted the growth of the legal profession, which attracted young, educated and critical middle-class intellectuals and provided juries with a chance to show their sympathies when faced with cases involving anti-Tsarist activities.**

The growth of opposition came about because Alexander II relaxed censorship **so allowing the works of radical socialist thinkers such as Nikolai Chernyshevsky, Alexander Herzen and Mikhail Bakunin to spread.**

The growth of opposition was the result of Alexander's reform of education and the universities **because the reforms gave the universities greater independence to teach the subjects they wished to and employ whomsoever they wanted as well as ensuring there was a larger student body which became receptive to new thinking.**

Page 17, Make the links: suggested answer

Reason	Comment and linking phrase leading to the next reason
The Narodniks were mostly upper-class students	who left their universities and homes in order to try to win the peasantry over to their socialist ideas BUT
The peasants did not understand the Narodniks	because their ideas were too intellectual and remote from their daily lives. They were suspicious of the students' activities AND
Peasants turned the Narodniks over to the authorities.	This undermined the movement and led to the arrest of 1600 Narodniks in 1874.

Page 17, How important?

	IMPORTANT	NOT IMPORTANT
Young Russia was probably behind a series of fires in St Petersburg in 1862.	✓	
Socialist writings had a minority readership – mostly students and the liberal intelligentsia.		✓
The St Petersburg Zemstvo demanded a central body to organise regional Zemstva.	✓	
Marxism was discussed in underground reading circles.	✓	
Peasants were suspicious of the Narodniks and sometimes reported them to the police.		✓
The head of the Third Section was assassinated.	✓	
Land and Liberty held discussions with the Zemstva.	✓	
Many members of the Black Partition were arrested from 1880 to 1881.		✓
The People's Will assassinated Alexander II in March 1881.	✓	

Section 2: Political reaction: social and economic change, 1881–1904

Page 21, Prioritisation: suggested answer

Most important   Least important

| 1 The government needed to modernise Russia and catch up with the West. | 3 If industrial development was to take place, the state had to provide the capital and incentive. | 6 The growth of industry could not take place without better transport links. | 7 By stimulating industrial growth, the state would generate more revenue. | 2 Better transport would lower prices and stimulate demand. | 8 More and cheaper grain could be sent to growing industrial centres and ports. | 5 Previously underdeveloped areas could be exploited. | 4 Both railway building and industrial growth would provide jobs (although not a prime concern). |

Page 21, Identify an argument

Paragraph 2 represents a high-level answer because it advances a supported argument. Paragraph 1 suggests a low-level answer because it contains only description and assertion.

Page 23, Complete the paragraph: suggested answer

Although the economic changes of the years 1881–1905 brought some benefits for the urban working class in terms of regular employment and wages, overall the working classes in the industrial towns and cities suffered more than they benefited. For example, **they often found themselves living in grossly overcrowded cities in poor unsanitary accommodation, the worst examples of which had no running water. Some had to live in barrack-style buildings provided by factory owners but even they were better off than those who simply slept beside their factory machinery. Industrial workers had little privacy, having to eat in canteens and wash in communal bath houses. Their wages barely kept pace with inflation and even if they managed to find a room in a private house, the rent might take half a week's wages, while the amenities were still basic. Long hours of work, lack of safety controls and exploitation at the hands of managers added to the misery of the urban workers. Although some welfare legislation was passed in the period from 1881 to 1905, there was no opportunity for workers to make their concerns felt since trade unions and strike action were banned.** Consequently, although increased industrialisation was ultimately to raise standards of living in Russia, in these early years of industrialisation, the working classes saw few of the rewards of economic change.

Page 23, Turning statements into reasons: suggested answer

STATEMENT	REASON
Russia's population had doubled in the second half of the nineteenth century	... because the profits of agriculture were insufficient to support a growing rural population.
Peasants lived in mirs, which collected their redemption payments	... because peasants were unable to travel and seek regular wages and improve their positions.
The government was committed to the promotion of industrialisation	.... because peasants were seen as expendable by the government, which was only interested in the promotion of industry.
Kulaks could afford to employ labour	... because since 1861, a gap had opened up between the wealthier peasant kulaks who took advantage of the less enterprising and bought up their land and the poorer peasants who became landless labourers.
Former state peasants were granted more land than the former privately owned serfs	... because peasants formerly in private ownership often had too little land to live on (although state peasants received more land and so fared better).
Peasant land banks were introduced in 1885	... because while loans from the peasant banks from 1885 helped the wealthier kulaks to make themselves richer, most peasants could not afford to take loans and if they did so, they merely increased their burden of debt.
America was able to export cheap grain to Europe	... because the primitive agriculture of Russia could not compete with cheap imports coming from the USA.

Page 25, Delete as applicable: suggested answer

The demands of opposition movements were **a fairly important threat** to the Tsarist governments in the years 1881–1904. The liberal intelligentsia's desire for a National Duma was **quite threatening** to the Tsarist autocracy while the aims of the radical opposition, which was divided between the Socialist Revolutionaries and the Social Democrats, was **very threatening**. This was because, **despite Tsarist repression, there was a growth in these opposition movements in the years after 1881 and the aims of the latter were a direct challenge to the autocracy. Whilst the liberal concerns for a National Duma undermined the idea of one-man rule, they did not directly threaten the Tsar or his government. The latter readily ignored the petitions and the society banquets of 1904, occasionally taking action, for example removing liberals from the Zemstva in 1900, but mostly content that the liberals were of little consequence. The socialist opposition was more threatening in its aims, which included the remodelling of society and abolition of Tsardom. The Socialist Revolutionaries successfully carried out a number of assassinations, while the Social Democrats saw the future of Russia emerging from an uprising of the working classes which they sought to promote. Both used terrorist tactics but the exile of leaders and the split in the SD ranks all helped weaken these groups before 1904. Therefore whilst their aims were very threatening and, as a whole, the opposition movements were a fairly important threat, it cannot be said that they constituted a major threat at this time.**

Page 25, Long-term or short-term?

	LONG-TERM	SHORT-TERM
Martov wanted to co-operate with other liberal parties, trade unions and co-operatives.		✓
Plekhanov created The Emancipation of Labour – a Marxist association.	✓	
Lenin was a very ambitious and committed Marxist who believed he knew what was best for the party.		✓
Lenin wrote 'What is to be done?', emphasising the importance of workers' revolution over trade unionism.	✓	
Lenin's brother was hanged after involvement in a plot to assassinate Alexander III.	✓	
The Social Democratic Party's first congress was broken up and its leaders were arrested.	✓	
Marxism was able to spread through literature that was smuggled into Russia.	✓	
Lenin wanted a highly disciplined party of professional revolutionaries to lead the proletariat.		✓

Page 27, Eliminate irrelevance

Both Alexander III and Nicholas II tried to uphold the principle of autocracy and, for the most part, they were successful until 1904. Alexander III arrested 150 members of the People's Will and hanged those responsible for his father's murder at the beginning of his reign. Censorship and security were tightened ~~and the Tsar withdrew to his fortified castle at Gatchina in case there were further assassination attempts.~~ Alexander increased the powers of the police and used both gendarmes, recruited from the nobility, and the secret forces of the Okhrana to prevent opposition. ~~During Alexander II's reign, the populist opposition movement had emerged and then developed into Land and Liberty. In 1879 this had split into the two factions –the Black Partition and the People's Will.~~ From 1882, any area of the Empire could be considered an 'area of subversion' and the police could arrest, imprison and exile at will. In 1901, during Nicholas' reign, a group of mounted Cossacks charged a student demonstration, killing 13, while 1500 students were imprisoned. ~~Both tsars were advised by Pobedonostev who had highly reactionary views.~~ Alexander III appointed Land Captains from noble families in 1889. They partially replaced the local magistrates and Zemstva, which were considered too liberal. Peasant and liberal representation on the Zemstva was reduced, some trials were again held in secret ~~and Nicholas openly admitted that politics bored him.~~

Page 27, Creating a Venn diagram: suggested answer

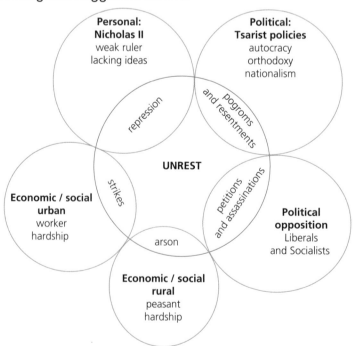

Section 3: Russia in revolution, 1904–1906

Page 31, Prioritisation: suggested answer

Most important   Least important

5 The war added to the high unemployment and raised the price of goods.	8 Blame was directed at army officers and government ministers.	6 Media reports inflamed the city workers and led to further blame.	4 Wartime humiliation suggested government incompetence in land battles.	7 ... and in naval encounters.	3 Conscription directly affected some townsfolk; others had family members in the army.	1 The humiliation was greater because of the Russians' low opinion of the Japanese.	2 Russians saw the Japanese as aggressors (but it was the failure to repel them that caused unrest).

Page 31, Develop the detail: suggested answer

Russia's wartime failures certainly contributed to the discontent that led to the outbreak of revolution in St Petersburg in 1905. Firstly, the war proved an embarrassing humiliation for the Russian state. **Port Arthur was subject to a long and inglorious siege ending in surrender in December 1904, 90,000 lost their lives in the Battle of Mukden in March 1905 and the entire Baltic fleet was lost in the Tsushima Straits in May 1905**. Secondly, it showed the chaotic nature of that state and how difficult it was to rule such a vast empire **that spanned two continents**. The Tsarist government could not run the war effectively. **It took the troops and supplies six days to cross from west to east along the single-track Trans-Siberian railway and it proved beyond the capability of the many different government departments and private businesses involved to co-ordinate the supply of weapons and men to meet demand.** Furthermore, the war created severe economic disruption which added to the discontent at home. **Imports and supplies to factories were disrupted and more lay-offs ensued, whilst inflation soared as the price of scarce commodities rose.** The workers suffered badly and this is what provoked the fatal strikes which helped to cause the 1905 revolution. Far from being the short victorious war that Plehve had promised, the Russo-Japanese War was a fairly lengthy and disastrous affair, which also brought about Plehve's own assassination in 1904.

Page 33, Long-term or short-term?

	LONG-TERM	SHORT-TERM
Because industrial workers had very poor living and working conditions	✓	
To present a petition listing workers' grievances to the Tsar		✓
Because there was very little welfare legislation to protect workers in the city	✓	
Because there was a strike at the Putilov works	✓	
To ask for working-class representation in government		✓
Because Father Gapon had created an 'official' trade union	✓	
Because the workers were loyal to the Tsar and felt Tsar Nicholas could and would help them		✓

Page 33, Delete as applicable: suggested answer

In the months between January and October 1905, political opposition was **only partially successful** in bringing about the revolution in Russia in 1905. Following the slaughter on Bloody Sunday in St Petersburg in January 1905, the more moderate liberals and national minority groups as well as the radical Socialist Revolutionaries and Social Democrats all sought to maintain the political agitation and press for constitutional change. There were strikes, uprisings, political meetings, petitions and mutinies in the following months, all fuelled by news of further disasters in the Russo-Japanese war. Before October 1905, the Liberals had **unsuccessfully** tried to **persuade the Tsar and his ministers of the need to grant a National Duma elected by the Russian people**. The national minorities had **unsuccessfully** tried to **press for greater independence**. At the same time the Socialist Revolutionaries had **fairly successfully** managed to **remove key political figures, such as Plehve by assassination** while the Social Democrats had **fairly successfully** managed to **win a following among the workers.**

The **failures** of the opposition were because **of the refusal of the regime to concede reform or even accept its worth and the repressive means that the regime had at its disposal, with the Okhrana and the army. Even though the radicals had enjoyed some success, the SD party split in 1903 and the arrest and exile of leaders weakened their ability to act.**

Page 35, Specific or underlying?

	UNDERLYING	SPECIFIC
Growth of opposition movements		✓
A general strike which brought the economy to a standstill		✓
Hostility to Tsarist autocracy	✓	
Discontent of workers and peasants	✓	
Zemstva demands for a full State Duma	✓	
Humiliation following defeat in the war against Japan	✓	
The unreliability of the army		✓

Page 35, You're the examiner

Level 5: This is a very well-argued and convincing paragraph that shows explicit understanding and an excellent grasp of precise detail. The candidate offers a well-balanced argument and shows judgement throughout.

Page 37, Make the links: suggested answer

Reason	Comment and linking phrase leading to the next reason
Workers believed the manifesto granted them the right to speak out, form unions and strike; the peasants believed it gave them the right to take land; the soldiers and sailors believed it gave them an opportunity to air grievances openly.	Consequently, the unrest continued and new demands were made for a wider franchise and further reductions in Tsarist power. Some wanted to see the Tsar removed altogether and they were attracted to the radical opposition.
The Socialist Revolutionaries and the Social Democrats wanted complete revolution, with social change too. Lenin and Trotsky tried to maintain the fight.	Encouraged by leaders such as Trotsky, who declared the Tsar's promises worthless, the politicised workers were increasingly attracted to the idea of a workers' revolution. However, this brought them into conflict with the authorities.
The army, police and the Black Hundreds were used to repress continued rebellion.	The repression brought violence and further unrest which was seen at its worst in Moscow. Bolshevik-inspired workers fought to the last there.

Page 37, Turning assertion into argument: suggested answer

The recovery of Tsarist authority was the result of the support given by the Octobrists and Kadets **who were prepared to accept the manifesto and call off their opposition, even though the latter saw it as only the first step towards constitutional reform.**

The recovery of Tsarist authority was the result of the November decree of 1905 which abolished the peasants' redemption payments **because this gradually helped to end the unrest in the countryside, although it took time before the peasant risings ceased.**

The recovery of Tsarist authority was because opposition groups were divided, poorly organised and inadequately led **as is shown by the division between the moderate liberals who accepted the reform and the radical socialists who did not, and in the failure of the St Petersburg and Moscow Soviets to co-ordinate strikes effectively.**

Section 4: The Tsarist regime, 1906–1914

Page 41, Spider diagram: suggested content

The Fundamental Laws

1 To rein back what had already been promised now the Tsar and the ministers were feeling more confident after reasserting authority in St Petersburg and Moscow

2 In order to by-pass the National Duma and so ensure Tsarist power was preserved

3 To prevent the revolution going any further and so resisting demand for far-reaching constitutional reform

4 To establish the position of the National Duma before the first Duma met in May

5 To clarify the Tsar's own position which was less defined after the October Manifesto

6 For religious reasons; Nicholas II believed he must preserve his God-given autocracy

7 To reassert command over the armed forces which was necessary after the mutinies of the previous year

Page 41, You're the examiner

This paragraph shows an awareness of context (although begins in an over-narrative way) and has focus. It explains and comments on some of the terms of the new constitution but it is very one-sided (e.g. it omits the crucial powers of the elected bodies to approve laws), offers generalist comment (e.g. the sentence beginning 'It was meant to...') and limited depth (e.g. in explaining 'autocracy'). It would therefore be placed in Level 3.

Page 43, How important?

	IMPORTANT	NOT IMPORTANT
Dumas could be by-passed, suspended and Article 87 used, or dissolved by the Tsar.		✓
Nicholas appointed his own ministers, who formulated laws.		✓
The third Duma debated, amended and approved important agrarian reforms and other government proposals.	✓	
The Tsar had to approve all laws.		✓
The Dumas acted as a channel of communication, allowing ministers to gauge popular opinion.	✓	
The franchise could be changed to control Duma membership.		✓
There was a growth of political debate as the Duma proceedings were reported in the press.	✓	

Page 43, Identify an argument

The first paragraph is from a low-level answer and is descriptive and assertive; the second is from a high-level response which advances a supported argument.

Page 45, Turning statements into reasons: suggested answer

STATEMENT	REASON
The years 1903–1904 were known as the years of the Red Cockerel.	... because Stolypin wanted to end the unrest of the years of the Red Cockerel (1903–1904) in the countryside.
Most Russian peasants had a very low standard of living.	... because he wanted to help raise the living standards of the Russian peasantry.
To encourage more peasants to move to towns to boost industrialisation.	... because he wanted to provide a mobile workforce to stimulate industrialisation in the towns.
Most peasants lived and worked communally in the mirs.	... because he believed that communal farming in the mirs was preventing the modernisation of agriculture.
Siberia was underdeveloped and sparsely populated.	... because encouraging peasant migration would enable underdeveloped lands, such as Siberia, to be used for farming.
1905 had seen violent agricultural as well as urban disturbances.	... because it would prevent further peasant involvement in anti-Tsarist political activity.

Page 45, Complete the paragraph: suggested answer

Although Stolypin's reforms changed patterns of landholding, helping to create a prosperous kulak class and leading to the development of large-scale dairy and cereal production in Siberia, overall they never succeeded in revolutionising Russian agriculture in the way Stolypin had hoped. For example, **the process of consolidating the land into individual farms with hereditary tenure proved to take even longer than Stolypin had expected and by 1913, only 1.3 million out of 5 million applications had been dealt with. Some landowners tried to hold on to their lands and it proved difficult to divide up common land without protracted legal battles. More conservative peasants, particularly in central Russia were, in any case, reluctant to give up the security of the mirs and around 90 per cent of farms persisted with strip farming. The poorer peasants who sold out to the more prosperous kulaks also found themselves worse off as they joined the ranks of the wandering labourers and slipped even lower down the ladder of poverty.** Stolypin's proposals were never given time to take effect because Stolypin himself was assassinated in 1911 and the war intervened to stop the changes in patterns of landholding which were underway. However, from the evidence available it would be certainly be untrue to say that Russian agriculture had been transformed in the years 1906 to 1914.

Page 47, Specific or underlying?

	UNDERLYING	SPECIFIC
A militant workers' movement developed from 1912.	✓	
The Lena miners had complaints about their accommodation, food and treatment.		✓
The Bolsheviks spread revolutionary propaganda and tried to co-ordinate strike activity.	✓	
Wages had not risen as much as inflation in the years 1910 to 1913.		✓
The miners' long hours and conditions of work in the inhospitable climate were grim.		✓

Page 47, Identify an argument

Paragraph 1 advances a supported argument. Paragraph 2 contains only description and assertion.

Page 49, Eliminate irrelevance

Although the Zemstva deputies had hoped that Nicholas would develop into a modern constitutional monarch, these hopes had not been fulfilled. Instead, the Tsar had grown increasingly detached, intent on preserving his God-given powers as expressed in the Fundamental Laws of 1906 and ignoring the complaints of the National Dumas. ~~Nicholas was a weak-willed man, who had never wanted to be Tsar.~~ Nicholas and Alexandra celebrated the tercentenary of the reign in 1913. ~~Nicholas and Alexandra held a spate of balls and dinners as well as travelling in great pomp across their empire, making a triumphal entry into Moscow on a white horse.~~ The praise he received reinforced his belief that he was loved by his people and that those demanding constitutional change were misguided. Nicholas also allowed Rasputin considerable influence at court and over Church and state appointments. ~~Rasputin was a faith-healer who appeared able to control Nicholas' son Alexis's haemophilia, but he was also a drunkard and a womaniser. Haemophilia is a disease that prevents the blood from clotting and Alexandra had become infatuated with this 'mad monk'.~~ Rasputin's corrupt influence undermined the Zemstva's hopes for a more democratic government still further.

Page 49, Develop the detail: suggested answer

In many ways the Tsarist government failed to restore stability despite the absence of any further revolution after the momentous events of 1905. There were four different National Dumas **in May/July 1906, February–June 1907, from November 1907 to June 1912 and from 1912 until after 1914** and this constant swapping and changing meant that the national government was far from stable. Each Duma had its own ideas and complaints and dealing with opposition took up a good deal of time. **For example, the first Duma wanted the abolition of the state council and ministers responsible to the Duma, while the second was highly critical of Stolypin's agrarian reforms.** There were many different political parties too, **ranging from the SD Mensheviks and Bolsheviks to right-wing nationalist parties** and they all had their own ideas about the different issues the Dumas considered. There were also Tsarist ministers, **such as Goremykin and Stolypin,** who had their own separate views **and were hostile to any Duma criticism.** Government was therefore unstable and it was hard to get much done. In addition there was lots of unrest among the broad masses of the population. The peasants were not satisfied with the **agrarian** reforms that were attempted **by Stolypin, which were slow to take effect and which did not make life better for all**, while the industrial workers became even more militant **as seen in the Lena Goldfields strike of 1913.** Government almost broke down in the last few years before the war which was a sign that the Tsarist government had not been very successful in restoring stability.

Section 5: The First World War and the revolutions of 1917

Page 53, Creating a Venn diagram: suggested answer

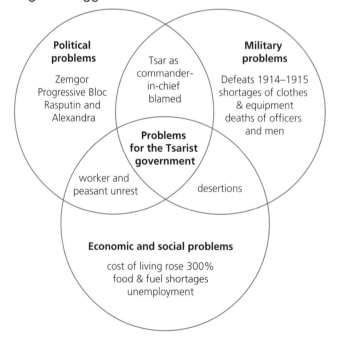

Page 53, Delete as applicable: suggested answer

Military failure was **the most important reason** for the weakening of the Tsarist government in the years 1914 to 1916. Despite the surge in Tsarist support that greeted the declaration of war in July 1914, a spate of battle failures and military organisational incompetence soon weakened the government. Early defeats and reports from the front line **made a huge difference to** the public's perception of the government from 1914 to 1915. It was Nicholas's decision to make himself commander-in-chief of the armed forces in September 1915 that **added to the already extensive discontent which had accompanied the 1914 defeats at Tannenburg and the Masurian Lakes. As commander-in-chief, Nicholas was held directly responsible for the wartime effort and although the army was better equipped by 1916, its lack of trained officers and an efficient Russian railway network to move reinforcements to the front line meant that it suffered a string of humiliating reverses. Furthermore, Nicholas' absence from Petrograd permitted Rasputin to increase his influence and for Alexandra, as a German, to be blamed for 'selling secrets to the enemy' and encouraging Rasputin's corrupt ways. The failure of the Brusilov offensive was compounded by the breakdown in trust for the government and the heavy casualty toll in 1916 left the Tsarist regime in an extremely vulnerable position as the opposition mounted.**

Page 55, Make the links: suggested answer

Reason	Comment and linking phrase leading to the next reason
Factory closures and disputes had put a lot of men on the streets at the time of the International Women's Day march on 23 February.	They seized the opportunity to join the women and to persuade others to join the strike. There were plenty of citizens ready to protest.
The working classes in Petrograd were in a desperate economic situation. Adding to their down-trodden pre-war position, the war had brought a huge rise in the cost of living.	Women from the bread queues, striking female textile workers and militant students all had good reason to protest. Even some soldiers became mutinous and the crowds shouted revolutionary slogans encouraged by the demands of the national Duma.
The military effort, under the command of Tsar Nicholas II, was going badly and the Duma had demanded the Tsar's abdication.	Consequently, the crowds swelled and by Saturday 25 February Petrograd was virtually at a standstill with over half the capital's workforce on strike and an escalation in vandalism and violence.

Page 55, Specific or underlying?

	UNDERLYING	SPECIFIC
Nicholas was a stubborn but weak man with little idea of how to rule his vast empire.	✓	
The Duma had grown exasperated with Nicholas' failure to appreciate the significance of the Petrograd riots.		✓
The Tsarist government had missed the opportunity to transform itself in 1905.	✓	
The Russian war effort was disastrous.	✓	
The army generals lost faith in Nicholas and the armed forces mutinied.		✓
Nicholas allowed Alexandra to influence him and gave Rasputin (up to 1916) and Alexandra too much influence over the Petrograd government during the war.	✓	

Page 57, Prioritisation: suggested answer

Most important   Least important

5 Land-hunger had long been the peasants' main concern.	4 Requisitioning deprived them of food and the opportunity to make money.	8 Many peasant families were affected by conscription.	6 The peasants had expected immediate change after February 1917.	2 The slowness of the PG suggested the peasants would be forgotten about.	3 Peasants could not understand why no improvement came about.	1 Some were encouraged by agitators, especially socialist revolutionaries.	7 The peasants did not appreciate the need to wait for a constituent assembly.

Page 57, You're the examiner

This paragraph represents good Level 3 work. It is knowledgeable and accurate but there is no direct reference to 'Dual authority' and, even more importantly, no attempt to consider 'how important' the relationship between the Soviet and Provisional Government was. Although it has some suitable detail and links to the question, it lacks weight and depth, tending towards description rather than a balanced evaluation, as would be needed for Level 4.

Page 59, Spider diagram: suggested content

The April Theses

1 To win support by saying what Russians wanted to hear: peace, ending the war; bread, giving food for all; land for the peasants; power to the Soviets

2 To unite the Bolsheviks under Lenin's leadership: provide a statement of intentions; end co-operation with the Provisional Government; challenge the leadership of the Provisional Government

3 To highlight the inadequacies of the Provisional Government: failure to end the war; failure to manage the economy; failure to stop unrest

4 To extend Bolshevik appeal: associate Bolsheviks with a popular programme; associate Bolsheviks with a strong leader; challenge SRs and Mensheviks

5 To spread Marxist-Leninist ideas: win over the proletariat with belief in revolution; promise a better future based on the forces of history

6 To accept what was already happening to the land: acknowledge peasant ownership; accept dispossession without compensation

Page 59, Turning assertion into argument: suggested answer

The deteriorating economic situation was largely the result of wartime dislocation because **the diversion of resources into the war effort forced non-military factories to close due to a lack of raw materials and fuel. Furthermore, escalating food prices were partly the result of the disruption to agriculture which followed conscription, the diversion of grain supplies to the front line and the invasion of Russia by German troops.**

The continuation of war helped to radicalise the peasants, soldiers and workers because **the peasants bore the brunt of conscription and grain requisitioning, the soldiers (mostly from peasant stock) were being forced to fight a war they did not believe in and were being commanded by officers they did not respect, while the workers suffered from rising prices and unemployment.**

It was the failure of the Russian June offensive that led to the July days, which challenged the Provisional Government's authority because **it was followed by thousands of desertions and heightened frustrations, particularly in Petrograd, home to the Kronstadt sailors, and brought soldiers, sailors and workers on to the streets.**

Page 61, How important?

	IMPORTANT	NOT IMPORTANT
Trotsky controlled the Red Guards.	✓	
The Bolshevik Party had grown rapidly during the summer of 1917.		✓
Large numbers of Russians favoured a soviet takeover.		✓
The strategy employed on 24–25 October 1917 was very successful.	✓	
Lenin continually urged the Bolshevik Central Committee to take action from mid-September.		✓
The Provisional Government was very weak and had few defenders.		✓
Trotsky suggested making an uprising coincide with the Second Congress of Soviets.	✓	
Trotsky was Chairman of the Petrograd Soviet and one of the leaders of the MRC.	✓	

Page 61, Long-term or short-term?

	LONG-TERM	SHORT-TERM
The failures of the Provisional Government necessitated a new style of government.	✓	
Lenin wanted to establish an exclusively Bolshevik government.		✓
It was essential to set up a new government without delay in order to address Russia's problems.		✓
The Petrograd Soviet in 1917 had been dominated by moderate Mensheviks and Socialist Revolutionaries.	✓	
Lenin was determined to establish a body that could rule by decree without going to the Soviet.		✓
Lenin did not believe in power-sharing with other socialists.		✓
The Bolsheviks had split with the Mensheviks because they favoured a strong professional leadership and a less democratic party.	✓	